Challenging

by
Jane Patricia Campbell

Copyright © 2021 Jane Patricia Campbell

The moral right of Jane Patricia Campbell to be identified as the author of this work has been asserted in accordance with the Copyright, Designs and Patents Act of 1988.

All rights reserved. No part of this publication may be reproduced, stored in a retrieval system, or transmitted in any form or by any means, electronic, mechanical, photocopying, recording, or otherwise, without the prior permission of the author and copyright owner of this book.

This is a work of fiction, all names, characters, businesses, places, events and incidents in this book are either the product of the author's imagination or are used fictitiously. Any resemblance to actual persons, living or dead, or actual events is purely coincidental.

ISBN: 9798485963774

This book is dedicated to all those who have ever had a hand in my life good, bad or indifferent.

Trust in him at all times; ye people, pour out your heart before him: God is a refuge for us (Psalm 62:8)

Dedicated to my dear children, Soumia, Kayla & Felix the puss!

"Put it all in the sea of forgiveness... and forgetfulness."
Grandpa Arnold

Prologue	5
Part 1	7
Everything Comes From God	7
Chapter One	8
The Interview	8
Chapter Two	15
School Days Filled Me With Shame	15
Chapter Three	19
We Were Dirt Poor	19
Chapter Four	24
I Was The Only One To Be Beaten Like That	24
Chapter Five	28
Sexually Abused By Lloyd	28
Chapter Six	32
Surviving My Childhood	32
Chapter Seven	43
Searching For The Real Me	43
Chapter Eight	49
Adam	49
Chapter Nine	55
At Last I Had It All	55
Chapter Ten	60
Money Doesn't Always Lead To Happiness	60
Chapter Eleven	64
Ill Health Became A Part Of My Life	64
Chapter Twelve	70
Telling My Children I Was Going To Die	70
Chapter Thirteen	76
The Lord Reached Out To Me	76
Chapter Fourteen	83
Everything Began To Change Once I Had Faith	83
Chapter Fifteen	87
God Sends The Hardest Battles So We Can Heal	87
Part II	97
My Redemption Years	97
Chapter Sixteen	98
Finding My Way Through The Wilderness	98
Chapter Seventeen	103

Reflections	103
Chapter Eighteen	109
My Bible Study Class	109
Chapter Nineteen	114
I Lost My Faith In Him	114
Chapter Twenty	118
Life In Jamaica Before I Was Born	118
Chapter Twenty-One	126
A New Life In England	126
Part III	131
The True Meaning Of Love	131
Chapter Twenty-Two	132
The Generational Curse In My Family	132
Chapter Twenty-Three	139
I Learned The Importance Of Forgiveness	139
Chapter Twenty-Four	146
Healing The Past	146
Chapter Twenty-Five	152
Support From Old Friends	152
Chapter Twenty-Six	163
The Joy Of Sisterlocks	163
Chapter Twenty-Seven	168
Jesus Will Always Be With Me	168
Epilogue	176

Jane Patricia Campbell

Christians understand God to be all good, and goodness often makes enemies. Good people, sometimes even by their quiet demeanor in a room, may affect the behavior of others. This presence of goodness, whether in a person or spiritual may thwart deceit, seem to run interference on questionable activities, or impact the tone of conversation. This can leave some people feeling peeved and pressured.

I was handed a tract or golden ticket, leaflet about Jesus, Repentance, Baptism and being Holy Ghost filled never imagining in sixteen weeks my burdens lifted after several outpourings of tongues – which changed my life. Prior to that I lived in shame, condemnation and was totally lost. It seems unbelievable now that at the initial stages as Bishop sat with me, as to why I was so reluctant, with the Evangelist words 'Gods knows the heart'.

Are you living under condemnation? Are you weighed down by guilt and anxiety about your past? Maybe you have done things which would embarrass you if they became public knowledge. You may have a criminal record or a moral charge or a domestic conflict that, to this moment, is private information. You may wrestle with a past that has been fractured and wounded by a mental or emotional breakdown. Futile attempts at suicide may add to the previous scar tissue and increase your fear of being labelled "sick", "nervous", the mad one or crazy. It's possible you live with memories of an immoral relationship, a financial failure, a terrible habit, a divorce or a scandalous involvement. You may be your worst critic of your past.

From John 7:53-8:11, we can learn how to overcome condemnation.

1. Let him who is without sin cast the first stone …

Conviction is from God (accept it); condemnation is from Satan (reject it).
Conviction leads you to repentance; condemnation drives you to despair.
Conviction inspires you to keep striving; condemnation tells you to quit.

Coping strategies:

Stay silent or, when people are quick to condemn us or criticize us, set a boundary with them. Ask them, "Have you ever committed a similar sin? How did you feel? Would you have wanted them to remind you of that or put you down in front of others?" When you are being attacked, it's better to take the offensive than be defensive.

Better still, bless them and remain silent. Always with a smile.

Prologue

The Lord is close to the broken hearted, and saves those who are crushed in spirit.
Psalm 34: 18

I have followed many paths in my lifetime and somewhere in the *Challenging Seasons* my spirit became lost. Until, after many years, I learned to place my trust in God.

My parents were first generation West Indians who came to England in the nineteen sixties. Mom-mi would often repeat Grandfather Arnold's words: "Life has a way of whipping people into shape." And he was right! I was ostracized, despised, and regarded as the black sheep of the family. After being abused, and beaten as a child, when I struggled later with cancer, I reviewed the experiences of my life, loss of home, former divorces, role of single parent, and being left in crippling debt. It was a constant battle coping with my mental health; suicidal thoughts, depression, and a lot more...

When I asked God to help me, I began to change my beliefs about the past, and the generational curse from which many families suffer and reviewed our own. I was eventually able to forgive, and find peace in the realisation that He hadn't stopped reaching into my heart across the years or loving me. Despite the difficulties I faced, I wasn't alone. Nor had I ever been.

I began writing this book many years ago, stops, starts, pauses, bits of paper here and there. It also helped me to heal. Gathering together a diverse collection of thoughts which told the story of a life with fiction. How I had to go through the darkness in Part I to find the light; for everything to change then in Part II, and lead onto me being happy, casting my cares on the Lord, through prayer, fasting and attempting to manifest a Christ like attitude – I am not a robot - I still make mistakes.

Challenging Seasons is a work of fiction, partly based on many events and experiences in my life. The people in the book are fictional but may reflect those I met along the way. Any resemblance to actual persons, living or dead, or actual events, is purely coincidental. I begin my story with the job I desperately wanted and believed at the time I deserved although God had other plans.

I wish you peace in the thoughts you have and many, many blessings. I hope you will be inspired by this story, the first in a series, and find it of help to you.

Much love,

Jane x

Part 1

Everything Comes From God

In the beginning God created heaven and the earth. And the earth was waste and void; and darkness was upon the face of the deep: and the spirit of God moved upon the face of the waters. And God said, "let there be light: and there was light."
    Genesis 1: 1-3

Chapter One

The Interview

My heartbeat quickened with every click of the heels on my new shoes whilst the ceiling towered high above me, making me feel even more insignificant than I imagined I was, but I didn't have a choice. I had come too far not to carry on past the dark brown doors and wooden paneling stretching endlessly ahead. Capped and gowned images stared down at me from the walls. As the fan heater I walked past blew the ends of my scarf, slithering it down to my waist, I checked my Rolex again before adjusting the flimsy material and took a deep breath. I had done it!

On my last visit to Lindsey House in Lincoln's Inn Fields, I stood looking up in awe at the imposing buildings. There were a lot like this in London but I hadn't expected to be invited to go inside one of them. The House itself was built in sixteen forty. I had read about it, together with all the different Inns of Court and Barristers' Chambers which belonged here. I did a double check. Stop, right there! I had to stay calm and not get too excited. I ought to have learned by now to quieten my thoughts, not to let them wander too far. I wasn't sightseeing today. Nevertheless, a shy smile couldn't help but remind me how much I loved this new world I was entering. The Barristers and Solicitors rushing between the Inns of Court in their cloaks, caps, and gowns pulling trolley dolly suitcases in ubiquitous black; with folders and contrasting red ribboned papers in abundance, they scurried about their business.

Another ominous click of my heels on the flagstones and I was inside the waiting room, sparking interest from seven sets of curious eyes, seated on two rows of sturdy metal chairs which had been lined up uniformly against the walls. "Was I the only black person to be interviewed?" The voice inside my head insisted that I ask the question, but thankfully I knew that I couldn't do it. I took a seat instead on the edge of the room, as quietly as I could, joining the other candidates in examining our formal surroundings. Everyone was dressed immaculately in expensive suits and leather brogues shining black or brown with Wall Street style haircuts that were clearly intended to inspire confidence. An ornately carved wooden desk separated us from the receptionist. Her manicured fingernails tapped efficiently on the keyboard. Her clothes said that she was fastidious. If I hadn't known otherwise, I would have thought, from the dark blue skirt which fell demurely to her knees, that she was also here for an interview. My thoughts could no longer be restrained and erupted mercilessly from beneath my carefully controlled appearance. "Lord have mercy!" I said, anxiously under my breath, not actually intending to be heard by anyone, but things never seemed to work out as I planned.

The receptionist quickly glanced in my direction and appeared to sniff at me before using the desk to push herself up out of her seat. Ignoring my feeble attempt at starting a conversation with her or anyone else in the waiting room, she stared through me as if I hadn't spoken. My thoughts told me quite sternly not to laugh while the dry dusty smell inside the room did little to alleviate its stilted formality. Trying to divert my attention from what I had just done, and avoid any other faux pas, I bit my lip hard. Praying as soon as I had done it that it wouldn't bleed, I stared intently at the gold framed photographs on the walls. There wasn't a cap, gown, or anyone of colour hanging in the rows of faces which surrounded us.

All of the candidates were sitting bolt upright as if they were ready to leap to their feet, and make a charge for the door. None of them spoke, or made eye contact with anyone else. I knew then that this was serious competition, and I couldn't laugh. I was about to have my last shot at success. The sacrifices I had made to reach this point seemed unreal. Not only did I desperately want a pupillage in this particular Barristers' Chambers, I needed it, and Hell, I was going to get it! Whatever it took! I was prepared to do it. I had prayed; cried most days, and told no one else what I was intending to do next. Except Mom, as we sat alone in the carpark at Asda last night. The burning desire inside of me, to be the successful applicant, turned to sweat on my forehead and I reminded myself again to stay calm as my thoughts twisted and turned inside my head.

The Lord alone knew how all this was going to turn out! Trying to get parked in Lincoln Inn Fields an hour ago hadn't been the beginning of today's nightmare. I had fought every step of the way to get here. The competition was fierce and there weren't many positions like this to apply for. I couldn't even begin to count the cost of it. All those long nights spent studying, debts waiting to be repaid, and the effect it had on my children. I was behind again in paying the mortgage and utility bills. So, sitting here, and being the only black face in the room, really was the final straw.

"Ryan Wilson?" The receptionist asked the candidates. "Mr Wilson?" She repeated the words more loudly in a clipped tone, making it perfectly clear that we understood, before waiting for the tall man next to me to leave his seat. A crimson red tie on top of a white freshly ironed shirt added to his air of confidence as he strode across the carpet towards the room marked: "Interviews." Several minutes passed before he came out again, looking complacent. "Good luck, Guys" he said, strolling past us. I could tell that he didn't really mean it. The way he almost skipped from the room reminded me of how my Father used to go into the church across the road from where we lived, and the little bit of confidence I had left began to disappear. "Jane?" "Jane Barrett?"

"Yes! That's me!" I shouted at the top of my voice, interrupting the receptionist in mid-flow. Clutching my briefcase tightly, I strode past her towards the door, with every eye in the waiting room on my swaying hips and ass. I knew I looked good, and I was about to prove that they weren't the only asset I had.

A tall, well-built gentleman ushered me through the door. "This way please, Ms Barrett." As soon as I edged past him, I was met by a panel of two men and one woman. They rose almost simultaneously from their seats to greet me with a smile. I still cannot remember what happened in the first few minutes of the interview. I was completely in the flow when I talked about my work experience; the skills I had which were necessary for the job, and finally produced the documents they needed to see.

"Jane" the female interviewer said, breaking through my robotic presentation and putting my papers onto the table in front of her, "Could you please step out of the room for a few minutes while we make a decision?"

"Yes, of course," I managed to say coherently. Sometimes, if I became too excited, I talked very quickly and the words were indecipherable. I stood up, trying to control my enthusiasm as I grabbed my briefcase and retraced my steps to the door.

"The other door please, Jane. We aren't finished with you yet!" The man who said it sniggered. His words fell ominously in the space between us, before I was ushered into a smaller room by the first non-descript man. I was being kept well away from the other candidates. *What had I done wrong this time?* Panic surged through me, mingling with disbelief and anxiety about the last forty minutes. If only I could forget everything that had happened to me, at least for the time being. It was spoiling the present, again. The voice inside my head repeated the question more loudly. *What had I done wrong this time?* Why had I been separated from the other candidates? I tried desperately to go through everything I had said, and done. What the heck had just happened? I was sitting alone on a leather sofa in a small dark room. Something must have gone badly wrong. My reasonable inner voice was quietly telling me to breathe deeply; the interview panel didn't know what was going through my mind as I stood in front of them. I was in the clear. They had no idea of where I came from, or what had happened in the past.

A man's voice startled me. "Jane, please come in and take a seat." I must only have been in the small room for a few minutes but it felt like an hour. The sunlight hurt my eyes as they struggled to adjust again to the brightness inside the interview room. The woman was sitting by herself on the edge of the desk, beckoning me to come closer. She had long blonde hair and wore a light grey jacket with a black skirt. She was probably in her mid-thirties, younger than I was. I sat on the seat in front of the desk and wondered why she was being so casual.

"How did I do?" I asked timidly, whilst my thoughts screamed at her, "Just hurry up. Tell me!"

She looked at me and smiled. "Well!" Her silence followed this single word while I waited eagerly to hear what the panel's decision had been. "As you may have seen from the waiting room, we have a plethora of suitable candidates for the position." I lowered my head to stare at my carefully painted toe nails poking through my shoes. She leaned towards me, and rested her hand on my shoulder. At this juncture I had reached the point of barely being able to breathe.

"Jane, the position is yours!" Her voice broke through my thoughts, causing the pupils of my eyes to double in size when I looked up. My heart was pounding so hard inside my chest I felt as if it might explode.

"Are you for real?" I shouted unprofessionally in my excitement, almost immediately recoiling my head into the back of my neck like a turtle does when being attacked as I realised what I had done.

Still smiling, she looked into my eyes. "Yes, it's for real," she said, kindly.

Part of me still couldn't believe it. I jumped out of my seat, unable to contain my excitement and I thanked her profusely. "You won't regret this," I said, determined to make her proud of my achievements as a pupil and trainee Barrister.

"You are very welcome, Jane. We will contact you with a start date," she said, more sedately as she smiled at me again.

Oh, my Lord! I was ecstatic. "Thank you, God. Thank you so much!" I said as quietly as I could to Him, looking up at the ceiling when I was back in the hall again. I made my way back to the main door in a dream. The tall man who had ushered me into the interview walked quickly towards me. "Congratulations," he said, putting his arm around my hip and leaning across to kiss me on the cheek. With his head still close to my ear he whispered, "I am looking forward to seeing you again." Feeling bewildered I found myself walking side-by-side with him to the door, his hand still on my hip, making me even more uncomfortable. When I reached it, I tried to turn around to smile at the woman who had interviewed me. She was by this time walking behind us but he blocked my line of sight. Looking me up and down, he gently bit his top lip and scrutinized every centimeter of my figure before I was able to escape. *It was exactly the way Lloyd used to look at me!*

Walking back to my car, I pursed my lips in the way my abuser had done years ago, anticipating what was about to happen. Except this time I could sigh with relief, as every click of the heels on my shoes increased my excitement. Lloyd couldn't hurt me again. I was no longer a child and my life had finally changed for the better. This was the beginning of a new chapter, all of my hard work had paid off although I couldn't help but still have a niggling doubt. Did I truly deserve this success? I hadn't been the best child growing up and I most certainly hadn't lived as a saint when I became an adult.

As I opened the car door a scuffle broke out between two children nearby. I didn't understand back then why people fought, and I still don't. I have never wanted to hit anyone despite being punished severely when I was young. There was only one occasion when I did try to defend myself and even then I wasn't successful.

I soon made myself comfortable inside the car, and put the pedal to the metal. The sun was still out, making the London streets aware of its presence. Its yellow rays bounced from building to building lighting up the road like a Highway to

Heaven. I was homeward bound with the radio on, Beyoncé increased my happiness tenfold. It was more than time for me to get a break. I couldn't stop smiling. Whilst deep down I also couldn't forget that life hadn't always been as good as it felt right then.

Chapter Two

School Days Filled Me With Shame

It was a warm morning, I was six years old, and about to start primary school. Mom-mi was holding my hand, albeit too tightly, as we walked past the school fields. When I stared at the grass bank which the older kids slid down on pieces of cardboard, she didn't hesitate in pulling me closer. It was as if she knew my attention had wandered into how much I would love to be able to do this. "Will you stop dawdling, Patricia!" she muttered angrily under her breath, so that none of the other mothers and children would hear. Except me. "You know I have to get to work!" Her grip on my hand tightened.

Given that she used my second Christian name I knew it would be best to do as I was told. I didn't want anything to spoil today, especially not being punished. So, I tried instead to think about what a wonderful time I was going to have with all the other kids. My face had been vaselined, and my afro hair was as neat as it could be; I was wearing white knee length socks. The hand-me-down shoes on my feet were scuffed but shiny. I looked down in wonder at them while I tried to keep up with Mom-mi hurrying along the path. It was easy to be distracted by the reflections I could see, as the sunlight caught them. The monster which looked like a giant dog, similar to the one owned by our neighbours whom I had learned not to get too close to. He growled if I went anywhere near him, and had bitten my sister a couple of weeks ago. We really loved to antagonise him and let him chase us….

My small fingers stroked the dress I was wearing. I was so proud of it. Mom-mi had sewn it by hand. I had watched her cut the material out before turning it magically into a pocket dress. Just for me! I had been told to cover it that morning with my sister's purple and black fur coat despite being far too large for me. Grace was older than I was but nothing was wasted in our house. Mom-mi was fond of saying that everything had a purpose, even if it did look old and worn out. She had turned the sleeves over so that they didn't cover my hands completely but the fur had a mind of its own. It had already started to fall down. Even though this felt uncomfortable, I was not accustomed to having anything new, so I still felt like a princess from a fairy tale that morning. I was very excited, and I didn't know what I had let myself in for.

I was also a caramel skinned kid. You could say I was lanky, certainly tall for my age, and I was black! Number three in a family of five. Apart from Grace I had two younger sisters, Juliet and Elsey, and an older brother. My skin was a little lighter than my youngest sister Elsey. She really was jet black! and became the beauty of the family. That's all my elders said and we youngers ones repeated it. Mom-mi knew as soon as I was born that I was going to be different. She had often said as much. When I pushed my way into the world, I was pure white, with ginger hair and freckles. She said I had a bright pink mouth edged with broad lips which I kept open day and night crying.

As soon as I saw the door to the classroom at the end of the path, I became even more uncontrollable. I pulled away from Mom-mi to run the rest of the way there. I waited triumphantly with my hand on the door frame until I saw the frown on her face as she huffed and puffed after me. Mom-mi was a very large lady who easily became breathless. Fortunately, her features quickly rearranged themselves when the teacher appeared in the doorway, and the two women greeted each other as old friends. I already knew that Mom-mi had given Mrs. Bates a perm a few weeks ago. She had been inside our house and seen the chaos in how we lived. She spoke kindly to me. "Hello, Jane! How lovely to see you. Welcome to your new school." I grinned at her as she ushered us inside, and showed me where to hang my sister's coat.

Again, without waiting for Mom-mi or my new teacher, I barged into the classroom feeling great. I looked around at the other girls dressed in pink, white and yellow skirts. I saw nice shirts with matching cardigans; white socks encircled their ankles in frills, and they had the shiniest shoes I had ever seen. I had played with these girls every day in the street outside our houses, but they looked amazing in their school uniform. Most of them also had small cases decorated with cartoon characters. I learned later that these had biscuits, crisps and pop inside. I thought at first that Mom-mi must have forgotten to give me mine. But she had left shortly after I went into the classroom so I couldn't ask her for it.

It wasn't long before Mrs. Bates told us to sit down quietly, as I was the last one to arrive. No one said anything about my dress, although I did catch a few of them looking sideways at it, as they shook their long plaited hair and ribbons before taking a seat at the table. I tried to wave to my best friend Angelica but I couldn't attract her attention. The other girls also continued to ignore me. After only a few minutes, I could feel myself shrinking into what seemed then to be the size of a grain of sand. I had been looking forward so much to going to school, and for once being the centre of attention in my new dress. I didn't understand that, despite the amount of punishment I received at home, intended to turn me into an obedient child, I still came across to others as a know-it-all, when the reality was I didn't know a lot, except about chaos. The other children were by this time giggling happily with each other. They had turned away from me to examine each other's clothes in great detail, and their cases of coloured pens.

I stared at Angelica who was engrossed in conversation with another girl, and it hit me later how I must have appeared to them that morning. I was loud, I didn't have the right clothes; quite simply, I didn't fit in. They must have realised it too. No one spoke to me at all on my first day at school except Mrs Bates. As if the situation wasn't bad enough, small flakes of dust started to fall without warning from my hair onto the table. When I looked closely at them, they wriggled, determined to draw attention to themselves. I had only seen them previously on my bed sheets so I wondered what they were doing there. I quickly brushed the table but it was too late. The others had seen what I was desperately trying to hide. They began nudging each other and sniggering behind their hands.

In that same moment, jealousy's green eyed monster raged within me as I stared defiantly at their jet black, sleek, textured hair which had been thickly coiled by doting mothers. Bobbles and plaits were in abundance, adorning their beauty with the prettiest of ribbons. I couldn't help but scowl at them, especially Angelica. Part of me wanted to touch their hair but thankfully the tiny voice inside my head told me not to try to do this. I looked down at the table instead when I realised that even their clothes smelt nice. Every single item of their outfits matched, from the green cardigans they wore to the bows on their shoes. *They had everything I didn't.*

A few weeks later when it was almost the end of term, the day our class was going to the beach arrived. I went to primary school wearing only my knickers and a dirty grey vest. Mom-mi had refused to buy a backless dress for me like the ones the other girls were wearing. Not only that, I had misunderstood what was going to happen that day. When I strolled into the assembly room everyone was singing, "Morning Has Broken." I can still recall the shame and humiliation the child within me felt as I took my place alongside them. I didn't have any idea then that the situation could get any worse, but it did. I found myself walking down to the medical room later that day, covered in angry spots which had erupted on my legs, face and the other parts of my body I had mistakenly exposed on the beach. I had chicken pox, and was by this time inconsolable.

Chapter Three

We Were Dirt Poor

After a while I discovered that one of the only places I felt safe as a child was lying in Mom-mi's bed. Every morning when she got out of it, I would quietly scurry into her bedroom, to starfish across the sheet and blanket. I had very little space in the bed I shared with my younger sisters so this was a luxury. There was nothing else in the room which was important to me as a child. Luminous yellow flowers were pressed into the butterscotch wallpaper whilst cobwebs dangled from the ceiling.

A shiny dark wardrobe took up most of the space. It reminded me of a wooden coffin which was so large that it was impossible not to have it somewhere in my line of sight. There was a cot too, and only a small window which couldn't make the bedroom light and airy. Suitcases were overflowing with an assortment of clothes, and a huge barrel contained more of my parents' possessions, their best clothes, pots, and pans, even an axe and a sickle. The lid still had labels on it from when the barrel travelled from the Caribbean, and a corroded metal rim which was also intact. Some of these things had been used in Jamaica so had become treasured, but were of little use in England. They just lay there in the barrel, abandoned, perhaps too as a reminder of what once was?

Unsurprisingly, what I found the most comforting in Mom-mi's bedroom was the aroma from her linen sheets. They had a strong scent of lavender and roses. I could lie there, almost believing I was in a meadow surrounded by beautiful flowers. Sadly the daydream didn't last for long; it was usually interrupted by the bang of the front door and the chatter of visitors, neighbours, family members and friends who had come to get their hair done.

The front room where Mom-mi did the hairdressing was directly underneath her bedroom. Dad-di liked bright colours so it was painted fluorescent green on one side and neon red the other. Enormous leather seats took up the entire room. I used to run down the stairs when I heard the first visitor arrive with the intention of sitting on the floor, in the corner between the two black bin bags which Mom-mi kept there, to watch what happened, and the others who would come in afterwards without knocking. Some of them were strangers but they still plonked themselves down on the variety of chairs dotted around the room as if it was their home too while they waited for a haircut.

Meanwhile, my Mother charged from room to room in her spaghetti stained shirt, occasionally picking bits of left-over food from in between her breasts and eating them, as the smell of sweat and hair gradually filled the house. When I followed one of her customers into the kitchen, it wasn't unusual for me to slip in the trail of water dripping from the woman's head. Parts of the kitchen were also used for hair styling; blow dryers had been bolted to the dining table and a cracked mirror taped to the wall. Holding my nose to try to limit the unpleasant aroma which became stronger as the morning wore on, I would pluck up the courage to pester them.

"You want me fi roll your bald?" I asked, clutching a pair of clippers. "And how about you?" This short stint of questioning was mostly interrupted by a wallop around the back of the head, and me sitting down again in the corner without saying another word, fascinated by watching Mom-mi work her hot and steamy, alchemy. The iron dipped in the blue magical oil she used. Twisting the tongs expertly in her hand she would separate hair into sections then delicately create neat, glistening curls. Women and girls would leave our house smiling and looking beautiful, leaving the squalor we lived in behind them.

The hairdressing sessions usually went on for several hours before the last customer left with all the hair having been rolled; permed and wigs collected. "Gwarn in there, me style ya out." Mom-mi used to say then as she made her way to the large, purple chair in the kitchen she liked to sit in. "Move outta me weh," she often shouted, slamming like a bowling ball through the crowd of children in front of her. "Gwarn to the chipper," she would say next when she remembered her maternal duty, pulling a thick wad of money from between the spaghetti-stained breasts. We soon learned to take one of the notes from her hand and run gleefully to the chip shop.

At six o'clock in the evening, Dad-di would come down the stairs. This was the earliest we were allowed to see him because he did the night shifts at work. I would often run to him and take his hand, pointing at the door, trying to lead him outside to the silver gate. "You wan fi paint for a liccul while?" he would ask me, grabbing a tin of paint. Painting this gate was the only thing we did together. I loved every minute of it. On the other hand, if I could tell he was going to beat me, I would fly through the two glass doors at the front of the house, and hop over the same gate. By the time I was at school it had become my favourite sprint! Otherwise the gate was left wide open after we had finished painting the bottom part of it. "You gwarn inside now. Let the gate dry out," he used to say, and I would hurry into the house, laughing and closing both of the doors behind me. When I turned around again, I could only see his outline through the window.

Even now I cringe sometimes when I remember the outside toilet we used. It was red brick tiled with a green painted door and a latch handle which didn't close properly. It was bitterly cold too during the winter months; you could see between the slats into the yard, looking through the gaps at the brown gate into our garden, and Dad's attempt at a vegetable patch. The people who lived opposite had built an extension from which they could look directly into the toilet. I used to crouch down to avoid their prying eyes, with my backside in full view. When it was dark, the lights from their house shone through the slats, so that we could see what we were doing. There often wasn't any toilet paper so, with my legs apart and pants pulled half-way down, I used to leave the toilet and traipse through the kitchen and living room. No one batted an eyelid when I did this. I climbed the stairs as quickly as I could to look under Mom-mi's bed until I found the toilet paper among the dust, carrier bags full of sheets, sanitary towels and odd shoes. There was no point looking in the bathroom next door; the outside toilet was always given priority. The stench of urine from the one indoors made my eyes water, coming from my youngest sister's terry towel nappies soaking in there, or simply piled up waiting to be washed.

Stepping over Patch, the cat who liked to lie on the black drain cover, was often part of the process in going back to the toilet through the garden. The ground had been partially slabbed but it was in reality a mish-mash of concrete. A pebbled circle for the clothes line was in the middle. There was also a passageway leading out to the street and around to the front door. We often climbed up the passage wall; it was covered in grime and cobwebs. On one occasion I fell off and I knocked myself out. Mom-mi gave me some black love that day when she saw me lying on the ground unconscious. This involved being whacked with a wet mop until I got up again. Taking me to the Accident and Emergency department at the hospital didn't cross her mind. "You'll live!" she roared at me, before stomping back down the passageway to watch Crossroads on the television.

The garden next door was immaculate, a complete contrast to ours. The roses growing along the wall had the most wonderful scent. The elderly couple who lived there pitied us, but still didn't like our ball going into their garden, perhaps this wasn't surprising. We would usually take the opportunity to steal their strawberries, or something else that caught our eye, causing some damage or another. Their large brown dog growled at us but lay still; he was much better fed than we were. We didn't stroke him, or have a proper conversation with them. When the woman spoke to us, she usually said, "Don't let the ball come over again!" Not that this stopped us.

The house on the other side of them had a large brown shed with a square glass window. One day while we were swapping one chicken leg for one chapati with the children who lived there, we started to throw the ball to each other and broke the glass. No one was surprised when this happened. As first-generation kids we mostly hung out on the street. We used Coca-Cola cans as shoes as soon as we discovered that they would stick to our feet if we stamped on them when they were empty. I remember the boys also making something wonderful from four small wheels, a plank of wood cut in two, a few nails and a bit of string. All of it magically transformed into a go-cart without any brakes.

We didn't need to worry about traffic interfering in our games when we played outside as no one had a car. We enjoyed knocking at another neighbour's door so that the big black poodle who lived there would chase us. The corner shop at the end of the street catered mainly for Asians and Jamaicans. It was crammed full of all sorts of things in what appeared to us as children to be an Aladdin's cave. In reality some of the goods must have been rotten or nearly so, and it smelled awful. It was impossible to see clearly what was on sale. Meat hung beside sacks of potatoes, boxes of yams and green bananas. Despite this it still had the best five pence and penny selection of sweets in the world if you held your nose to get past the smell, squeezed around everyone else inside, and the strange languages they spoke while bartering for ten Park Drive cigarettes.

Chapter Four

I Was The Only One To Be Beaten Like That

It wasn't unusual for Dad-di to be rolling dumplings when I came into the kitchen after school, helping Mom-mi before he went to work. I used to squeeze behind him to open the wooden cabinet which was divided into three sections, with orange doors in the centre. The bottom part was usually padlocked because the food was kept inside it, whilst the middle section opened up to create a surface for buttering bread. In front of the crockery which was piled high, there was a large dish used for butter along with an accumulation of black ants, old toast and unknown chunks of something or another. The ants were an everyday hazard, crawling through the butter. We learned to pick them out, and carry on as if this didn't matter; also, to ignore the rat trap in the corner of the kitchen. "Cum outta me way, pickney!" Dad-di used to say to me, telling me to move aside, as I watered down the milk to make it last longer.

I suppose it was inevitable that, as I grew older, I became louder, ruder and more challenging at school. Mom-mi's way of dealing with this was to tell the teachers to give me the pump whenever they wanted to, provided Dad and her were not called into school when they were at work. She took this one step further when I went to secondary school and thought it might be a good idea to separate me from the local kids. What a big mistake that turned out to be! I was bullied from the outset, excluded and isolated. These kids were second generation, their parents were young, educated, western and up-to-date. They had gone well beyond the first generation of those born in Great Britain; just like me!

After a while, in a desperate attempt to fit in, I bullied another girl from the petrol station into getting sweets for me. I teased her shamelessly about her body and newly developed breasts. I only did this as a way of trying to fit in but it didn't make any difference. I wasn't the same as the others. My hair was plaited while they had curly perms, chemical perms and jerry curls, with stone washed jeans, rara skirts and fur coats. I still had hand-me-downs. Their clothes were tight, and modern, freshly changed short skirts, frilly blouses and different versions of another uniform. Meanwhile I wore an old-fashioned flared skirt, and one stiff, light blue shirt which smelt awful, given that I wore it every day. I was out of my depth with these kids and I soon learned to enjoy my own company. I occupied myself on my own. I stood alone in the playground as they smoked or walked to the chip shop and flirted with boys.

Life at home was different again in our overcrowded house. I can see now that Dad-di was trying his best to live as he had done in Jamaica through that tiny patch of garden at the back of the house, growing potatoes, cabbage, carrots, runner beans and tomatoes, with only his green shed and a few tools from home. His eyes often told me how much he missed the many acres his family farmed in his childhood home, Jamaica. It was easy to see that he was lonely; he was very quiet, rarely speaking in public. Only the church opposite our house seemed to give him any comfort. All he did was go to work and come home again. He didn't have any friends or eat a meal with anyone else. He didn't even read the newspaper like most other men did, although he liked to listen to the news and cricket on the radio and television set at the same time. He had a small stature with dark brown skin. Mom-mi would dye and cut his beautiful white and grey hair so there was always a black shade around his hairline and moustache. He was an agile man, fast and strong, supporting Mom-mi one hundred per cent in whatever she might say or do.

I soon learned that his beatings were ferocious, sharp and precise, delivered without fail when I answered back, often for what seemed a minor thing like not fetching this or carrying that when I had been told to; also especially when I played music too loud. If it could be heard in the church opposite during the service, Dad-di hit the roof. We could see his reflection then through the glass doors before he came into the kitchen without making a sound. He didn't shout or give any warning of what was about to come, unlike Mom-mi who would cuss first then wallop me, or throw the nearest thing to her. I thought at the start that everything was okay because he didn't show any outward signs of anger.

I carried on with what I was doing until he unexpectedly grabbed and held my body against the wall as the sharp pain from his blows continued. He could even manage to unbuckle his belt, with its two centimeter width, as he held and lashed out at me. The pain from the belt was excruciating, sharp and short, again and again. Only then was I told what I had done wrong, in the midst of my flesh being on fire, burning raw, trying desperately to draw itself in to avoid any further punishment, instead stinging, bright red. When he had finished, he would put his belt on and go back to the church, as if nothing had happened.

I was the only one in the family to be beaten like this, believing it was my fault because I had answered back, challenged what I was told to do, or had quite simply been cheeky. My siblings watched as Mom-mi literally stood on my back in her bare feet. She would carry on punching me, with her entire twenty-four stone weight on top of me. I used to try to curl myself into a little ball, covering my face and making the silliest of noises. As Mom punched, kicked and whacked me, I howled and said ridiculous things in an attempt to end the punishment, whilst my brother and sisters laughed. Mom-mi didn't like a lot of noise and often became distracted by it. When she started to get tired of what she was doing, I managed to do my famous sprint. I had also learned by then to do a Mohammed Ali shuffle with my feet, put up my small fists as best as I could, then run well away from her while my entire body screamed in pain and confusion.

When I was older and still being punished by Mom-mi, Dad-di and I fell into a routine. He sat in the chair nearest to the kitchen waiting for me to shoot past him, run through the two rooms and out the front door, jumping over our silver gate. He used to follow me but once I had escaped he would go back inside. Being treated in this way, I found it easy to bully my youngest sister Elsey, staring at her until she cried, and making her repeat how everyone told her she was the darkest. We didn't have conversations in our family about how we felt, nor did we hug. No one said sorry and we didn't have any emotional hang-ups about what was happening; we simply didn't talk about it afterwards. We also didn't have any days out. It was always clean up, eat up, shut up, and play outside. The only goal I had while I was growing up was to get an education so that I could afford to have my own house.

Angelica and I used to talk about it although she wasn't punished by her parents in the same way as I was, she said that she wanted to live with me in my imaginary house. The plan was we would marry each others brothers, thou they completely ignored us, instead more focused on body popping and spinning on their heads. We would have lots of fun, amongst other things, being able to play music as loud as we wanted to... But then, there was him! My abuser, whom I believed was the tallest man alive. *He lurked in the shadows until it was time for him to come for me again.*

Chapter Five

Sexually Abused By Lloyd

He was almost ten years older than me, and easily twice the size. The short sleeves of his shirt tightly hugged his bulging biceps. His skin was incredibly light for a black person, so much so that he could almost pass as Caucasian. "Me come ya, Jane." I remember him saying to me, with that look on his face. He was coming to our house so I knew what to expect, and that it would begin by him staring at me when my parents went out.

"You better behave," Mom-mi used to bark at us before she left. "If Lloyd tells me you nah done what he want, I'll shatta you a couple licks when me come home!" The message from this was perfectly clear. I had to obey him, and do what he said or I would face another beating. "Ba-bye now," she shouted, as she slammed the door behind her, not realising what she had done.

Her departure was followed by shouts of joy from my brother and sisters as they proceeded to run riot. Sprinting upstairs, they soon disappeared without any objection from the person who was supposed to be looking after us. Perching himself on the edge of the couch with his legs crossed, he stared in my direction. "Jane, why not mek mi sumfin fa eat," he said, licking his thick, crusty lips.

The first time it happened I happily hopped into the kitchen. As I brushed past his legs, he patted my bottom and whispered, "Good girl, Jane!"

The kitchen didn't hold many options from the point of view of food. The cupboards only contained a variety of dead ants and cobwebs, but half a packet of stale bread on the counter caught my eye. "I know, I'll make you a sandwich," I said, determined to do as he had asked. I had short legs which made it difficult to reach up, and get any food which might be there. Balancing on tiptoes, I attempted to grab the bread. It had been shoved to the back of the counter against the loosely tiled wall. A loud slap on the door frame caught my attention and I turned around immediately.

Lloyd was walking towards me grinning. He stopped a couple of feet away to lean against the wall. His left knee was slightly bent as he placed the sole of his foot against the crumbling red paint. He slapped his knee, slowly bringing his hand up to his face, to stroke the stubble between his nose and top lip. Leaning forward to reach the bread I could feel his eyes on me, looking me up, and down; pursing his lips outwards, he made sucking noises. "You are weird," I couldn't help saying to him, as I pulled the bread from the packet. "We need some butter and cheese next." Skipping a few steps towards the fridge, my hand reached up to open the door. I heard another slap which was much closer this time. Glancing up nervously, I saw him towering above me. With one hand pressed against the fridge and the other rubbing his belly, his fingertips dipped rhythmically into his jeans.

"Let me get it," he said, grumbling when it seemed that he would have to stop what he was doing.

"I can do it. I have my special step. See!" I said, pointing to the plastic box on the floor, still trying to be helpful and at the same time escape from being trapped underneath Lloyd's right arm while his hand was by now gripping the edge of the fridge.

"Me no want food! I've changed my mind," he said, in a tone of voice that didn't expect to be challenged.

"Well, what would you like?" I replied, again trying to do as Mom-mi had told me to, not realising how tantalising this question might be to him.

Looking me up and down, he started asking me questions. "How old are you?"

"I'm eight, I'll be nine in October," I said, proudly, as he moved his hand from the edge of the fridge and put it on my shoulders.

"You are a big girl aren't you? Do you know the difference between big girls and boys?" he said, leering at me.

"Boys have big shoulders and are very strong," I replied, innocently, not understanding what was happening when his hands moved quickly down to the backs of my legs, and he lifted me up against the fridge.

"Like me?" He asked, lifting me up even higher with my back against the fridge as he moved closer to me. I will never forget the onion on his breath, mingling with the foul smell of his oily skin.

"Please can you put me down? I don't like it!" I said, starting to panic. Ignoring my plea, the grip around the back of my legs tightened. "Let go!" That was all I managed to say before I remembered Mom-mi's stern warning about the consequences of being disobedient. His head dipped behind mine, and he inhaled deeply as he smelt my hair.

"Mmm, strawberries and cream," he whispered.

I heard a stampede of footsteps, seemingly a long time afterwards, as my brother ran down the stairs. "He's coming! He's coming!" Delroy shouted when he reached the bottom step, before he burst into the kitchen followed by my sisters,

Lloyd tossed me carelessly onto the floor as soon as they appeared. "Silly bitch," he muttered to himself.

I felt myself starting to bruise almost immediately. I rubbed my knees which had taken the brunt of the fall. Lloyd looked down at the red marks on them. "Don't forget what your Mother said. She shatta you a couple licks if you don't do what I say. Me say you nah speak ah dis, understand?" He said, reminding me of what might happen if I dared to disobey him and told anyone what he had done.

"Yes Lloyd," I said quietly, not wanting him to say anything at all about my behaviour to Mom-mi.

"That's my girl, Jane," he said, gently, in an attempt to make sure that he had persuaded me. He put his hand on the top of my head to ruffle my hair. I felt confused and very sore; something wet was running down my leg. Lloyd had hurt me and I was crying as I fumbled my way into the dining room. Dem kids was so happy, I attempted to shake it off.

Chapter Six

Surviving My Childhood

A few years later, I wished I had known karate back then and been able to stop Lloyd. I had started to watch Bruce Lee movies with my siblings and practice the moves he made. Reaching the bottom of the stairs, I would often be greeted by a karate kick to the chest. "HWAAAAA," my brother used to shout, as he slowly brought his arms up into the crane position. "You have come to test the Master, I see!" Laughing, I would try to walk past him only to receive another kick, this time to my ribs, stopping me in my tracks. "You must face me in combat," Delroy said firmly. This playful fighting would be interrupted more often than not by a proper whack from Mom-mi, without saying anything, as she walked past. Just like a bowling ball in an alley, she could fly through a room, striking everything in her way.

Strangely enough, apart from being bullied and ignored, school could also be a lot of fun, especially when I became a bully too! I didn't see anything wrong at the time in what I was doing, it just seemed like childish fun taking sweets from one of the beautiful girls. I derived a lot of pleasure from it without any thought of how she might feel. After I had been doing this for a year, a rumour started that I was a bully. Another girl wanted this title and decided to claim it from me. Karma bit me in the ass that day when I had to face up to Kara. At thirteen years old she was more than five feet tall, with dark skin and an ever present group of followers cheering her on. "Three o'clock! Meet me at the school gates," she said, demanding in front of an audience that I should obey her.

I didn't understand what was happening at the time, and I can still remember grinning at her. "Sure," I said, unconcerned.

When three o'clock arrived, the entire school was waiting for us at the gate. "Fight! Fight! Fight!" they chanted repeatedly.

"Wait a minute! Who's fighting?" I asked the nearest ones to me in alarm.

"We are," Kara replied, with a smirk.

My heart sank as I quickly considered the Bruce Lee movies I watched every weekend, the moves Delroy had used on me. The spirit of Bruce slowly took over my body. My hands moved into the crane position and Kara stepped back in fear. "It's working!" The voice inside my head joyfully told me when I reached the peak of my stance, but before I could launch a devastating kick, Kara sprang from her back foot and gave me a solid right hook on my jaw. My dreams of becoming a karate Master died that day, along with my reputation at school, as I plummeted to the hard concrete floor.

I felt my head spinning. I have so many memories of my childhood. Even now, they still twist and turn through my thoughts. It was also quite clear that the community Church felt sorry for us. They used to bring food and clothes to our house when I was growing up or take us out occasionally on trips. One such visit was to St. Austell, Cornwall. I had a curly perm before we went. This meant I had to go to sleep with a plastic shower cap on my head. I had forgotten to pack mine so I used a Tesco carrier bag instead; it was crinkled, and noisy. I covered my hair with the bag in secret but was soon tipped out of my camp bed for everyone to see. If I hadn't used the bag, I would have left damp patches from my perm on the pillows. Needless to say, the rest of the kids thought this was hilarious.

Not having a lot as a child, I grew up understanding the value of money, especially given how poor my parents were, and the long hours they both worked to support us. When I became a teenager I was under strict instructions from Mom-mi about how I should collect her wages for working sixty hours a week. These came to forty-eight pounds. I was like a robot in all the coming and going I did back then, but my Mother trusted me completely. I knew that the money belonged to us so I dared to go and collect it for her. I used to walk confidently into the nursing home where she worked. It stank of urine and faeces but the office was clean. I remember the staff keeping flowery cups in there. I put my name next to my mother's when signing for her wages. The Supervisor also trusted me with the money but the people who lived in the home often stared at me as I walked past them. They touched my coarse hair and asked me who I thought I was to come striding in as I did. No one had taught me to knock politely on a door before entering a room. I guess I was seen by them as a curiosity but it was a great feeling to be trusted with such an important job. I was the only one in our family who was. Nobody else! Just me! I felt ten feet tall when Mom-mi asked me to collect her wages.

I also remember rushing home from school one day and an elderly black lady was sitting in Dad-di's chair, she was breathing heavily. She often coughed, drawing phlegm from her chest, and spitting it into a handkerchief. She was wearing a dark blue and cream dress which had multiple layers. A shiny slip had escaped from underneath one of them. Light brown pop socks, and moccasin leather shoes covered her feet. Her hair was thin, grey, and frizzy. There were dark patches on her face and forehead. Whilst the smell which came from her was indescribable, she looked exhausted, drawn and very ill.

Mom-mi introduced her while I carried on staring. "This is Gran Una. She has come all the way from St. Ann in Jamaica and will be staying with us." All I could think of was how dismal she looked. So this was my nan! My Mom-mi had a Mom-mi, but why had she not mentioned her before now? But perhaps it wasn't surprising, given that her words of wisdom were usually only dispensed or shared during a cursing or beating. When my backside was the one on fire, Gran, or Aunt Una as we also called her, lived for specific periods of time with each of her children, moving from one family home to another, so that all of us were given the opportunity of spending time with her. The only problem with our branch of the family was that we didn't have enough room for ourselves in the house, let alone a guest, so I was very angry when I discovered that she was to have my single bed.

Delroy had been thrown out of the house by then for refusing to contribute to the household and live by Mom-mi's rules. The constant beat, blasting reggae sounds, contrasted somewhat with the church congregation as the service was ongoing; also boasting to Dad-di that he knew a secret about what Lloyd had done to me and laughing about it during one of their arguments. Dad-di ended up sorting both of them out whilst I got my brother's single bed! My younger sisters still shared the double bed I had previously slept in with them. Now here was Aunt Una about to take the single one from me. "No way. Not my bed!" I shouted, as soon as I heard the news, in a futile attempt to overturn Mom-mi's decision. The reality was, I should have known better by this time.

Angelica, my best friend, came striding into the room with fresh Hungarian biscuits on daddies battered silver tray – he was fuming. Angelica, with her long Jerry curl hair, stood in between as both sets of parents went for me.

Aunt Una looked straight through me as if I wasn't there, and certainly didn't have any right to voice an opinion on the matter. Her apathetic, dejected and bewildered face stared into a place only the Lord knew where. Nevertheless, I still hadn't finished making a stance. "No way," was all I managed to say next. The fried dumplings Mom-mi cooked were akin to bullets. On this occasion I felt the full impact of their burned hardness when she threw them at my head. Too late to escape, Mom-mi followed this up by catching hold of my skirt, so that she could trap me in the corner.

"No pissing tail pickney cum tell me bout seh what!" she said, resolutely, as she thwacked my face repeatedly with her fist. "Have some manners!' she screamed at me, while I managed to get into my submissive ball position. I was cornered behind the door to the cupboard under the stairs, but I still attempted to roll myself up as far as I could, while Mom-mi's disapproval and disgust raised her patois to a new level. "Dutty, stinking, renkin pickney!" she continued, as I felt every punch she made to my back along with the full kicks she gave my face, head and stomach. I soon became breathless, sore and aching as a result of this onslaught.

I tried my best to catch her feet to put an end to it, but she was too fast. She had changed into Big Daddy, the famous wrestler we used to watch on the television. Finishing with her favourite move of plonking herself down on top of me, she rested her full weight on my small frame. Nevertheless this meant that she was getting tired, so I could take advantage of it. I knew that she couldn't get up quickly from this position and I managed to wriggle out from under her before sprinting through the door.

Meanwhile my sisters were laughing and shaking their heads at Queen on the television set, whilst Angelica swished her hair from side to side, unable to focus on whom or what. It was as if they were not part of what had happened and it was simply background noise to the music. I guess this was their way of dealing with the violence. All of us were, after all, only children. They couldn't do anything about what was happening so tried to ignore it, whilst I was feeling the full effect of the beating I had received, and the fried dumplings which had been solid as rocks when they hit the back of my neck. Nevertheless, I was only too grateful that I had escaped again. Once I had jumped over the silver gate into the street, I was crying bitterly about the way Mom-mi treated me. How much she had hurt me. However, I didn't have anywhere else to go so I sneaked back into the house that night to creep into the double bed with my sisters. None of us managed to sleep for long because of the lack of room, and Aunt U's continual coughing; she alternated from spluttering, wheezing and being sick then blowing her nose as loud as she could, before gurgling the phlegm into a bucket. All I wanted was for her to be gone so that I could have my bed back.

It was impossible to compare her to the grandmothers we saw on the television, or anyone else's for that matter. Those nans cooked lunch in large kitchens, baked biscuits and walked with their grandchildren to school while they ate sweets and held hands. Elsey used to sit bolt upright and stare at ours in disbelief before giving me a descriptive analysis of how she wheezed and took her inhaler. I didn't bother listening to this. I went into my fantasy world instead, usually with Angelica, to cut out pictures from the Argos catalogue of all those nice things we would like to have in our house. Later on I would sleep for a while in this imaginary house, only to be awoken again by Aunt U's inhaler pump and her phlegm being spat into a light brown bowl, which I would walk over in the morning as my youngest sister examined its contents.

It became difficult to forget what Lloyd had done to me, especially when I was very young, and the sexual abuse carried on for a long time, even after Delroy told Dad-di and I was given my brother's bed, I still sometimes awoke at night from the fear I felt in a bad dream about it. Losing the bed to Aunt Una seemed to make those dreams a lot worse. I don't know how he did it when we visited his house one day but Lloyd managed to separate me from everyone else downstairs. One minute all of us were running around, playing hide and seek, dashing from room to room, upstairs and downstairs. Then I was somehow in the back bedroom, alone with him.

As a child, I thought his house was posh, because the bedlinen matched the curtains. You could even see the orange and black swirls in the carpet. I laid on the floor to hide, not realising that he would come into the bedroom; no one had invited him to play with us. Before I realised what was happening and without him saying a word, he was lying on top of me. I could feel the weight of his body, and see him if I opened my eyes, while he grunted, and wiggled about. I couldn't move so I lay still, alternately looking at his hair then up at the ceiling. I could tell that what he was doing was wrong. He was very heavy, but I didn't say a word, even though I could clearly hear Mom-mi's voice saying, "Cum now, we goin!"

He stood up quickly after that, hurried to the door and left, once he had made sure no one would see him go. He didn't even have time to pull up his trousers properly. I rolled over onto my side as the other children burst into the bedroom while his semen seeped down my leg and I still didn't understand what was happening. All I knew was that I was wet but I hadn't been to the toilet. My back was hurting again and my vagina no longer felt itchy in the way it used to; now it was hollow, swollen and painful. I wiped it with a piece of tissue before pulling my pants up. I didn't say anything. I got up and joined the excited group of children.

I can see now that it wasn't only what was happening with Lloyd, I simply wasn't the same as the others in many ways. When I was eight years old, I can remember lying on Mom-mi's bed with my legs wide apart while she leaned in to give me the vaginal shave I had once every three weeks. Even at that age my face, arms, chest, and vagina were covered in thick hair which was coarse, dense and dark brown. Her bed was soft, and warm. I had to lie still on it despite Elsey also playing in the room, popping up from the side of it, and slapping my forehead when she did this. Her hair was thick and strong although it had a natural spring and curl, she wore it long. It was always neat, with Dudu plaits for when she was jumping about, she had the best hair. Even her plaits moved naturally as she walked and played. Mom-mi loved plaiting her hair; she would spend a long time doing it, flicking the comb and hair as she centre parted it, and pulling the bundle of hair to be plaited. I know that I gave my family hell at home but I loved them dearly. No one at school was allowed to hurt Juliet and my little sister - only I could insult and upset them with my words.

Mom-mi shaved my vagina with a special razor which was shiny silver and had a screw top. You had to open it, put the razor blade inside, then screw it closed again. I absolutely hated this razor! Mom-mi used to press down on my legs when she shaved the hairs from my vagina. I didn't ask her why. All I knew was that it made me itch afterwards. Also that once the hair had gone, it would be back again in three weeks. If only my parents had taken me to see a doctor, they would have found out that I had a hormonal imbalance which made me produce too much testosterone, causing me to have a deeper voice than I should have done, and excessive hair growth.

Many years later, I would be diagnosed as having too much estrogen. As a child however, at the end of every shave, I used to watch Mom-mi knock the shaver repeatedly to make my ginger hair fall out. I would pull my pants up as soon as she stopped shaving me, and it would itch like crazy. I soon gained the reputation of being, "a scratcher." When I scratched, everyone said that it made them feel itchy. Eventually I became so conscious of doing this that I would only scratch myself in private, especially my intimate parts which the razor had nipped. I still became the butt of everyone else's jokes, loud mouthed comments, and the scapegoat when things went wrong. I often heard people say, "You always scratching, and renk!"

Sometimes I thought that the attention I received because of it was cool. On those occasions I believed that any attention was better than none. Anything negative or derogatory about me soon became a good source of gossip, easily believed, and never questioned. *Looking back, my path to becoming the black sheep of the family was very quickly set in stone.* But as far as Lloyd was concerned, I didn't like any of the attention I received from him. It wasn't right, and made me feel confused. He found me one day when I was on my way to school; he lifted me onto his shoulders. While I sat bouncing on them, I collided with a post and fell onto the ground. I was crying so much afterwards that the teachers wanted to contact my parents. I knew that they would beat me if this happened so I started to laugh instead, despite being in a lot of pain. Dad-di was working nights and would have been asleep, Mom-mi was at work. I managed to keep up this pretence while the pain and confusion I felt inside hurt me the most. *I was only a child.* I didn't understand what Lloyd was doing and I needed help. He showed one side of his nature to others and hurt me in private. Everything seemed much worse after that day when I realised that he could find me anywhere, even at school!

I used to hear Delroy telling his friends about Lloyd and

laughing with them during the conversations they had about girls, whilst I couldn't tell anyone else about Lloyd. I felt too ashamed. Angelica used to look at me strangely when she heard my brother talking to the others, but she didn't say anything. We always hurried past them to avoid any trouble. There was no one I could talk to, even if I had felt able to. I knew I was to blame, in the same way as when I was beaten by my parents.

I used to think that my life would get easier once I was older, but it didn't. There was always something waiting to go wrong. "Whose is this?" Mr Riley said one day, when the children in my class at school were getting into teams in the sports hall. "Whhoossse is this?" He repeated the question more loudly, stressing the syllables, his accent sharper, making certain that we could hear him. The chatter slowly subsided as we scrutinized the end of the rounders' bat he was holding in front of him. My dirty, soiled pants that I had worn for a week or more were dangling from it, covered in skid marks and urine stains. They were yellow and orange in places, interspersed with splodges of brown-black feaces. My dirty pants were being held up for all to see! I had to listen then to his unrepeatable description of them. Nasty was one of the words he used whilst my face was on fire from the shame of it. All I wanted to do was to run as fast as I could to the changing room. I had instead to listen to everyone else's laughter. One or two of the children slapped or punched me on the back when I ran past them as quickly as I could, with the dirty pants in my hand.

I spent the rest of the day alone, behind the assembly hall, totally overwhelmed by the horror of what had happened, and again, the shame I felt. We didn't have any fancy, lacy, printed white pants in our house. We had to use whatever we could find, often wearing the same socks, blouse, and vest for a week or more. Yes, of course, it smelt to high Heaven! We had Palmolive soap for washing and showering, but there never seemed to be any of it left. The tar soap was for washing the dishes. We also didn't have any deodorant but there was always Vaseline or cooking oil which could be used discreetly. If we couldn't find a comb for our hair, we used a fork.

I desperately wanted to smell nice when I was growing up, mostly of Persil washing powder; also to have the latest oversized men's shirts that I could wear on top of high waisted jeans with multi-coloured socks and a wide leather belt around my waist. I wanted my Argos catalogue kitchen to become a reality with its matching crockery, tiles, pots and pans. Angelica and I were going to have it all. We spent a long time sticking and glueing images from that catalogue, of how our new home would be. Every room had been carefully thought out. My dream was to have a bed covered in a beautiful quilt, with matching curtains and a carpet. Instead, from that moment on, everyone at secondary school thought I was not only covered in spots but was also dirty and smelt awful. Every time I walked down the corridor, I received a punch or slap. It was the same when I was walking home. I gave up trying to defuse the situation, and I occasionally fought someone who went too far with the abuse.

I discovered that fighting a bully was easy if he or she was alone, but this didn't often happen. They usually came for me in large groups, and one of them would only be friendly towards me if he or she had also for some reason been excluded. To get back into favour with the group, the excluded one created a scene which again involved me being bullied. Any attempt by me to flip the script and become a member of the group didn't work.

It was the same at home, I couldn't escape. I have so many bad memories of what happened there across the years, memories which have since come and gone from my thoughts in no particular order or chronology. "Why don't you just shuuuuuut your mouth, you pissin tail pickney? Why you always got to argue back? Why you got to say something? Why YOU?" My brother shouted angrily at me one day, as he physically pushed me down the narrow staircase. Delroy had a volatile temper. He had mastered the ability to catch me off guard. His fingernails around my throat were razor-sharp and encrusted in dirt. We were standing on the small landing, ten steps up from the hall below, next to a wooden banister that was dented and well worn. The last three steps had a curve on them which led into my usual battering corner. The family coat hanger was hanging above them, overloaded with old and new coats. The shelf above was filled with shoe boxes containing medicine. Needless to say, the carpet was threadbare. Some of the steps had been overlaid with a different one, to hide the worn out sections.

And here I was, literally being thrown down those stairs. I don't know exactly how it happened. I got caught midway, falling lengthways then, and giving my brother the opportunity to kick me in the back, making sure I experienced the full extent of his abuse and pain. Words cannot describe the hollering I did as I tumbled down those stairs. When he ran quickly down the stairs in front of me, I tried to get up again, only for him to catch my leg and drag me down backwards. I was pulled face downwards. I hit every step as punch after punch rained down on my body. When I was screaming for help, my breakdancing brother simply hopped over me.

"Born of the water, spirit, and blood. Thank God, I'm born again!" My older sister Grace sang, ignoring the commotion and praising God instead. She floated past us ethereally, apparently totally oblivious to the cruelty and abuse I was receiving from our brother.

By the time I was fifteen years old, I had been made to feel invisible; no one appeared to hear or see me. They definitely didn't care how I felt. I am not surprised that I was desperately lonely, ashamed and very angry inside.

Chapter Seven

Searching For The Real Me

When I left school in the eighties I joined the Women's Royal Army Corps (WRAC) in Guildford. It was formed in 1949 to make more men available for active service. Irrespective of them often serving with other regiments on long term attachment, the women in this section of the British army always wore a WRAC badge on their caps, and I was able to choose from more than forty trades in which I could later be trained. It seemed like no time at all before I was waiting to take part in my pass out parade. I made every effort that morning to put on my number two uniform properly, after polishing my shoes with a few good globules of spit. I had meticulously washed and ironed my shirt. Even managed to get my three inch baby afro hair into a tiny cornrow bun under my well-polished hat. I couldn't help preening when I looked at myself in the mirror. I was proud to be a part of this and I even felt a strong sense of belonging. The thought of leaving the barracks and Surrey countryside had been making me feel miserable for a while. I had learned to shoot a nine millimetre submachine gun, taken a physical training course and was being moved to the Catterick garrison to begin my trade training. However, despite all my achievements, none of my family had arrived to support me.

We stood on the parade ground which we had been taught to respect and regard as a sacred place. No one could take a shortcut or walk across it unsupervised. It was reserved strictly for training, practice, ceremonies and other important occasions when neat rows of young recruits like us, who had gone through the trials and tribulations of basic training, would stand to attention. We had been blessed with a warm day and I could feel the excitement in the air. Everyone had been looking forward to seeing their family and friends gathered together on the edges of the square, watching the roughneck kids they had brought up.

change before their eyes into refined; booted, and suited army personnel. Getting ready to move on to the next stage in their lives.

Night after night we had practiced on that parade ground, listening to, "Tallest on the flanks; shortest in the centre...." It was intended to be a wonderfully perfect display in the same way as it had always been done. Whether you saw a photograph of it in a book or in real life like on that day, the young soldiers always looked neat and tidy in their uniforms. When the taller soldiers were on the left and the shortest recruits in the centre, the right flank was expected to balance this in height. I was in the latter group on the front row. The mistakes we made when practicing had trickled back like dominoes falling, while the corporals hollered, using a variety of insults to get us properly in line. It reached the point where I could hear them and the shuffling of feet in my sleep. "Left; right, left; right," was bellowed repeatedly at us. As young raw recruits, we used to pound our feet hard onto the gravel, forgetting to swing our arms in rhythm or marching out of step with each other, we had a bawling out to get us to do it correctly next time. Even now I can't forget the jubilation I felt on the day we first saluted and marched as one. It had taken endless practice for all of us to reach that point.

I scanned the audience impatiently. Most of the people there were parents, and I was looking for a black face among them. My heart sank almost as low as my boots. *Surely someone could have spared the time to support me?* From under my bottle green peaked cap I carried on trying to make out where my family might be as we stood proudly to attention, mimicking penguins under the bandstand when the inspection began, facing straight ahead so that the parents could take photographs, whoop, point and follow our path around the edges of the square. Being careful to avoid walking ahead of the officers, and non-commissioned officers, I was one of the first to be inspected on the flank at the front.

The weather was glorious as we pounded our feet in unison, and saluted. This was it! Everything we had worked so hard to achieve. General Sir Peter Edgar de la Cour Debilliere walked towards us to examine the recruits. Although I was still some distance from him, my heart was beating in trepidation. I had seen a strikingly tall, overweight black lady from the corner of my eye. She was wearing a floaty blue printed skirt, striding and waddling from side to side with her twenty-four stone gut powering her through the crowd. Lord have mercy! She even had a new shiny, ill-fitting, brown and black wig. The fasteners were dangling down from the back of it. Give me strength! She was closely followed by my brother, Delroy, who had put so much gel in his curly perm that it must have been possible to smell it long before you saw him. My sisters pushed to the front of the crowd in their excitement, just in time to see Sir Peter Debilliere reach me. The other officers and parents stopped and stared as Mom-mi also nonchalantly barged her way to the front. She crossed her hands and grinned at me, revealing a large gap where her front teeth should have been. Muffled undertones could be heard while the examination was taking place, my sisters cooing and ah-ing.

Although I was very proud that my parents and family had come to watch the parade, I couldn't help but be proud they hired a car to be here. I kept my expression as calm as possible so that no one would be able to guess my feelings. Nevertheless, what had happened became the talk of the camp until the day I left. The reason why they were so late was because they had hired a car, set out in their old clothes and had to change in the guard room. As for Mom-mi's missing teeth, she had eaten some toffee, and lost them!

I joined the Women's Royal Army Corps as a fresh-faced teenager and any regrets I had at leaving it were soon forgotten. I set out to bury my loss in one party after another. With as much partying as I could get while I was travelling and living in London. As far as I was concerned every day was a party. I used to meet other service personnel and we enjoyed ourselves until dawn. Whilst this was happening I was also studying for my first degree in Business and Finance, often asking for an extension to hand in an assignment late, as I juggled my studies with work and parties. A short stint at modelling in a grotty Stepney Green Studio was even more of a hoot. One day I was taken out of a photo shoot, because I was not sufficiently "European." I watched the rest of it without saying anything. Although I thought quite a lot afterwards about how I could rectify this, the answer lay in piercings and tattoos, alongside a six month relationship with a lesbian lover called Jenny.

"Who, what eh!" Mom-mi said, clearly surprised the first time she saw us together. "This is your friend?"

"We are in a relationship, T-O-G-E-T-H-E-R," Jenny replied. so that my Mother wouldn't be in any doubt as to the way things were between us. Time stood still during the silence which followed while we sat in the squalor at home with Mom-mi giving us her very best vexed and hostile stare. This involved putting her neck back, with a hand on her hips so that she was standing akimbo. Jenny and I were sitting on the new leather settee with more glass ornaments than usual on the table next to it. My sister Elsey was holding two bright orange and brown glass cups in her hand. She slammed them down in protest but without attracting our attention for more than a couple of seconds. The living room was buzzing with vibrant colour; it had been painted yellow. There was a swirling red, brown and green carpet too. record player was on the sideboard, heavily decorated with white doilies. A large glass fish had been given pride of place at the centre, with Mom-mi's hair treasures safely stored behind it.

The Singer sewing machine was still crammed with boxes of hair, wigs, rollers, hot combs and wig bolsters. There was also an endless profusion of black bags wherever a space could be found to put one. Not a lot had changed across the years. Juliet walked in for dinner, followed by her friends from church. All of them were immaculately dressed for the service and had quite clearly heard the word: T-O-G-E-T-H-E-R. With her mouth wide open, she rolled her eyes and cursed under her breath. "Here we go! She turns up after years away and brings this piece of shit with her," she said, before storming into the kitchen to put the food on our plates.

We sat on the floor, and ate the meal in complete silence. No one mentioned it again or talked about it. Ever! The space on the floor that day was tight. It wasn't long before Jenny and I split up after I realised how much I was still attracted to men. I moved out of London for a while to start a new job as a facilities manager at three hospitals and I bought my first house in Aberdeenshire. I eventually moved back to London when I became employed by London Education Authority.

Late one evening I found myself hunting for a room at Ravenscourt Park in Hammersmith, London when I was mesmerized by the appearance of an elderly gentleman. I began talking to him. He was dressed flamboyantly, also heavily made-up, wearing bright blue and green eyeshadow. Our general chit chat turned to accommodation. It transpired that Marcus was renting a room in Shepherds Bush which he said I could take over if I wanted to. The building had a grand entrance. It was a white pillared property, with carved lions on the steps, and a huge glass door. There were black and white floor tiles, high corniced ceilings and panelled walls. The image of an elegant, and breathtaking apartment danced through my imagination. However, the reality was a little different. When we climbed the grand staircase, it soon became clear that there wasn't actually a separate room for me to rent. He only had one, with a sofa bed in it, an enormous grey elephant table, and a glass chair. All of it seemed to be clean. When I asked him again about the room, he said that I could have the sofa and he would take the floor. I thought it was a peculiar arrangement but it actually worked quite well.

Like most of the important decisions in my life, our agreement was made on the spur of the moment. I already had my bags and possessions with me so I could move in straight away. Whilst we chatted Marcus took a call, and mentioned afterwards that he had a friend called Adam who was going through a divorce in the High Court. He thought that Adam and I would get on well. He was apparently on his way to see us and the three of us could go out for dinner if I would like to. Marcus also asked me mischievously if I would like to have a date with his friend. Little did I know the huge impact this was going to have on my life.

Chapter Eight

Adam

What Marcus was suggesting sounded a little too good to be true, so I didn't take it seriously. I laughed and said, "Why not?" The answer came easily, just as if I didn't have a care in the world. The reality was that, less than twenty-four hours after moving into my new apartment, I was showering and getting ready to go out with two complete strangers. I wore a slinky black dress and six inch heels. My long, micro blonde box braids were down to my backside when I walked across the tiled floor. Marcus' friend had his back to the glass door but I could see his outline through it. He appeared to be slender and broad shouldered. Mmm, he was seriously good looking. I paused to stare. I could see that he was wearing a light blue shirt with dark blue trousers. When I opened the door, his eyes were the deepest blue of the sky on a hot summer day. Whilst his receding hairline only made him appear more distinguished, I knew it, right there and then, I was going to marry this man. I could tell that he knew it too. There was an instant connection between us, despite him being more than thirty years older than I was.

 I didn't bother telling Marcus that Adam had arrived. Why should I when I had everything I had always wanted standing beside me. Neither of us needed a third wheel. Instead I shimmied past Adam, slammed the glass door closed and started to walk down the steps. He raised his eyebrows and said, almost under his breath, "Fantastic!" before following me quickly down the stairs as I swung my hips and clicked my heels with every step I took. When his ancillary relief proceedings were concluded not long afterwards, we married two weeks later.

 I refused to sleep with him until after he had been introduced to my parents, and sat in the squalor of my childhood home. "Surprise!" I shouted across to him when he stopped his Porsche outside the house. He didn't say a word and was perfectly charming to my parents and sisters during the entire visit. "Rahted soup," Mom-mi said, using her favourite swear word to emphasise how she felt before we got back into the Porsche and off we went.

Adam loved this car. He drove it to Calais three weeks after we had met. I wasn't to learn until much later that he was possessive of everything he owned, but on looking back the warning signs were there. I had asked him a few days earlier if I could drive when we were going out for lunch. The frown on his face should have been enough to stop me. When I carried on trying to wheedle my way into getting his agreement he snatched the keys to the Porsche from my hand and slammed the front door behind him before getting into the driving seat.

I sat quietly beside him as he drove away, wondering what I had done wrong. Neither of us said a word, and I knew enough by then not to ask again, putting it down simply to how some men behave when it comes to their cars. Besides, the Porsche was out of my league, sleek and very expensive. What if I had damaged it? No! I had clearly been wrong to ask. Perhaps he may even have hated women driver,s or being a passenger, especially in his own vehicle? I hadn't a clue how to get out of the situation I had landed myself in so I forced myself to keep quiet.

By then I also believed that I loved him, and it wasn't long before I was in the habit of ignoring his moods. Much to my relief, he held my hand again when we stood on the deck of the ferry crossing the Channel. I remember thinking again, this is it! I have found the perfect man. His mood improved even more once he began telling me about the vineyard he would take me to on the way to Paris. He knew the owner and had bottles of wine from there shipped regularly to his house. He said several times that there was nothing better than sitting outside in the French sunshine, drinking a glass or two of red wine in the place where the grapes had been grown.

The problem was, it didn't stop at that. More like four or five bottles were drunk by Adam and Pierre, the owner of the vineyard, during the long conversation they had about the cost of making a single bottle of wine; the different types of grapes and their growing conditions. Finally, a drunken dispute occurred on whether French Champagne was still the best in the world! The more inebriated they became, the more bored I was. I had been looking forward to getting to Paris and having Adam to myself. I hadn't seen him for several days; he told me that he had been working late. As it wasn't the best idea for me to ask him again if I could drive, I sat quietly sipping the wine and trying to enjoy how beautiful the vineyard was, listening to their laughter in the background.

Pierre's wife was there too but we couldn't have a conversation. She didn't speak English and I didn't speak French. We smiled at one another at the start but she soon started talking to Adam and Pierre in French. Her soft laughter told me that she was enjoying herself when Adam had apparently said something funny. After the first few minutes, none of them tried to include me by translating what had been said; I couldn't help feeling miserable. Adam and I ended up staying at their farmhouse for the night until he was sober enough to drive the following day.

After a couple of hours he reverted to his usual self, considerate and charming. Of course I soon forgave him for ignoring me the day before and made a mental note that I had to accept I couldn't always be the centre of attention in his life. By the time we reached the outskirts of Paris, the magic was back, and neither of us could get enough of each other. He knew his way around the city as if he was travelling across London, so we were soon at the George V Hotel where he liked to stay, and had reserved a suite. I couldn't believe the opulence or the beautiful clothes which the women wore. I could tell almost straight away that mine weren't expensive enough for me to play the part Adam wanted me to. I soon felt as if I was an intruder. I didn't fit into this rich lifestyle, however much I wanted to. It was a very different world, far removed from the house where I had been born in Birmingham. Looking back again, at that first day when we arrived, Adam must have thought so too.

After a snack and some coffee had been sent up to the suite, he grabbed my hand. Before I knew what was happening we were in a taxi on the way to the district which sold designer clothes. My heart sank even further. I didn't know how I was going to tell Adam that I couldn't afford to buy even a small item from Chanel or the Jimmy Choo shoes I coveted, but I didn't need to. He kissed me on the lips in the back of the taxi, and gazing into my eyes, he said that it would be his treat. I could have whatever I wanted, provided of course that he liked it. I thought at first that he was joking about this, but it soon became clear he was deadly serious. When he spoke in French to the sales assistant who had brought an armful of clothes to show me, she turned away after a short "Oui, Monsieur!" only to return with different coloured dresses and separates a short time afterwards.

Despite thinking that I could handle any situation in my life, I was completely out of my depth although all of it seemed perfectly normal to Adam. I still wasn't used to receiving gifts, especially expensive ones. Nevertheless, after a few minutes, I realised what it was! He must feel the same way about me as I did him; it was true, love at first sight did exist, and this would be our happily ever after. I attributed the way he was behaving to him looking after me because I couldn't speak the language and he was very kindly paying the bill. We went to a luxury jewellery shop afterwards because he wanted to buy himself another watch. When he caught me staring at a gold bracelet in the display cabinet next to the counter, this was soon around my wrist. I genuinely believed by then that I was head over heels in love with him. When he turned on the charm, I had never experienced anything so wonderful, and there was even more to come. What was a few kicks, slaps and bruises.

A week after we arrived home, he called to see me unexpectedly and put a handwritten note in my hand. I was feeling stressed because I had to get to work, I was already late. He smiled when he told me not to worry about that. he would take care of it. The note said that I needed to pack a bag and be ready in an hour so that we could get to the airport in time for the private flight he had booked. When I looked into his eyes, I remember seeing only desire, and what I thought was a wish to make me happy. Without any more thought about what I was doing, or that I would more than likely lose my job, I did as he had asked, changing out of my work clothes into one of the beautiful dresses he had bought for me in Paris.

That night we walked hand in hand along the winding streets of Venice listening to the sounds of the gondolier in the distance and watching the green tinged light on the canals we passed. The restaurant Adam had chosen was full of Italian diners, not tourists. It had an old world charm to it similar to the Florian cafe where we had stopped earlier for coffee, and sat outside in St Mark's Square listening to the orchestra, until Adam wanted to leave. The bill was soon paid and I finished my coffee quickly while he tapped his new watch impatiently.

The restaurant he had chosen was wonderful. It was as if I had entered a fairy tale in which I had the starring role, alongside my Prince. I was even more certain of it when he took a small box from his pocket, opened the lid and slid the most beautiful solitaire diamond onto the fourth finger of my left hand. I was stunned as he went on to tell me where he had decided we should get married, and the house he had his eye on to buy for us. Adam didn't appear to need, or ask for my opinion, about any of it. Looking back, I should have seen the truth. I can't even remember if he doubted I would say yes. He simply assumed that I would, and to be fair to him he was right. Why should I refuse to spend what I thought would be the rest of my life with the man I loved? Or not want the fabulous change of life he was offering to me? I barely gave everything I would be giving up a second thought, the good job I had worked so hard to get and my independence.

Surely only a fool would refuse? Whilst this couldn't have been further from the truth, the foundations of our relationship weren't stable enough to sustain a marriage, certainly not children, and the cracks soon appeared. At the time I honestly believed that he truly loved me, apart from being swept off my feet, also because of the way he made love to me, the amazing sex we had. We couldn't get enough of each other! We just clicked. It was often the case that anywhere would do. Neither of us was able to wait any longer to satisfy our lust. I didn't know at the time that this was mostly about his need to possess and control the people closest to him or I might have had the strength to walk away. Then again, would I, especially at the beginning?

Chapter Nine

At Last I Had It All

So far as I know the first in Adam's stream of other women began twelve months after we were married. We had by then been on a lot of expensive shopping trips abroad and for holidays. He had also bought a Bentley. I loved St. Tropez, and the other European cities he took me to, like Rome and Prague. We always stayed in the Savoy or the Ritz when in London. Again, Adam liked their oldworld charm. I believe he thought of himself as a quintessentially English gentleman. The wine flowed throughout, along with the endless aperitifs and a good brandy after dinner, while his anger also grew, and the slightest annoyance or irritation could set it off.

Nevertheless, in those early days a contortionist could not have done better, with the sexual positions we attempted in his Bentley. Along the German autobahn and into St Tropez the ambrosial hours were heavenly in the late evening. When the sun was setting on the beach, a beautiful array of orange and red trailed into an inky night, sky. "Have you always been an ambivert?" He said to me one night when we laid side by side in bed on the point of falling asleep. "Professional at work, but extrovert and wild outside! I guess that's what drew me to you. I needed to meet you after a long marriage and a messy divorce." He turned his back to me then and began to snore.

I didn't know what personality traits I had. I am not sure I was even interested in them at that point. All I did was suck his penis, but I remember thinking a little drunkenly that I could get into this ambivert life. Not long after we arrived home and the memory of St. Tropez had time to settle, a slight unease began to creep into my thoughts. The alcohol had flowed when we were there, and the music played on. My new husband had shouted, "Let's balter!" waying to and fro with the notes. I realised then that I had no idea what he was talking about half the time but I went along with it, bumping and grinding to Chanka Music I was not familiar with, and still making excuses because I was very much in love with him.

A good marriage could have helped me heal the hurt and pain I had suffered while growing up. It's difficult now to believe that others were envious of the life I had back then. Most people thought of the big house we lived in with its sweeping drive, as they would have done winning the lottery. Also the spa holidays I had, with an endless stream of shopping trips to Dubai, St Tropez, Monaco, New York and so on. The new cars too, all of them were luxury brands, Jaguar, Range Rover, Bentley and Rolls Royce. I didn't have to work for any of it, but after a while I started to look at what I was doing with different eyes. Seeing it instead as a noose around my neck. I was often lonely and quite clearly by then at the whim of someone else's mercy. When he was happy I would be given money and allowed to use the car he had bought for me. However, if I had upset him for any reason, I was left alone inside his mansion house in the middle of nowhere, without any way of leaving it. Despite what I had always thought, I learned the hard way that having money didn't necessarily lead to happiness.

I actually began to miss the routine of going to work, seeing former friends, meeting friends for coffee, going to the theatre, just hanging out with my friends. Most importantly, I missed my home, my smells, my comfy slippers, my Laura Ashley settee and being in control of my own remote control.

All of the men in his group of friends had a multitude of ex-wives and vast material wealth. I thought this would be a lot of fun but it turned out to be incredibly boring. They often talked to each other in a monotone about the matrimonial disputes in which they were involved, the contact arguments they had with their previous wives about seeing their children, how much maintenance they paid, or the current cost of school fees. Not forgetting the other arguments between their children from previous marriages, and the new wives, mostly because we were often so close in age!

I would sometimes think back to when I had a life of my own before meeting Adam, even though it hadn't lasted. One particular day I was waiting to go into the staff area of European Airways at Paton Cross in London. I had applied for a strategic manager position, looking after a number of different departments and staff, including the company shops and catering section. The job involved a lot of responsibility, handling substantial amounts of money, keys to the premises and their customers, so I had not only to look good but needed the confidence and style they were looking for from an employee. It was a well paid job, but nothing in comparison to Adam's wealth. I had bought my suit from the Principles on Oxford Street. My two sisters, who were by this time students at Manchester and Durham Universities, came with me when I went shopping for an outfit to wear at the interview. I also treated them to some new clothes, shoes and a wonderful meal in Soho. As soon as I sent the train tickets to them, we couldn't wait to meet up.

The suit I bought was beige. It had a skirt, jacket and waistcoat worn with a white shirt. I thought at the time I looked great, but this was before the expensive designer outfits I wore after I married Adam. That day however, my long blonde box bead extensions stretched beautifully down my back. I wore red lipstick and glossy nail polish; five inch heels completed my glamorous appearance. I was single and sexy, five feet nine inches tall, size ten, and this was most definitely going to be my job. Three other candidates had also applied for it, two men and one woman. When it was time to go into the interview room, the white female was asked if she was Jane Campbell. When I called across to tell them that they were looking for me, they both stared. Afterwards when I was being shown into the room the interviewer said, pointedly, "This is Jane!" as if to send a secret message to the others who would be interviewing me. I could only guess at what that might be. They surely didn't know... *There were so many things from my past that I didn't want to tell them!*

I watched as they shuffled their papers, putting them into some sort of order before acknowledging me. The man who had shown me into the room stood up again and asked me to take a seat before the interview began. Each candidate had to give a presentation and use Excel to demonstrate that we could process data. We were expected to explain our findings afterwards, followed by lunch. I only took small portions of what was on offer and sat with the other candidates. The other female candidate took off her shoes and put them on the table, saying that she was tired, despite being in a crowded coffee lounge with company executives, pilots and directors, not to mention the interview panel members who were sitting nearby. Within ten minutes of her doing this, all of the candidates were ushered into a room and asked to wait.

The "I'm-tired-so-am-gonna-take-my-shoes-off" woman was sent home whilst one of the other candidates and myself were successful. Both of us were offered similar jobs in the north eastern and southern divisions of the company looking after the retail shops and restaurants, also managing a large cross section of the company's staff. We were told that putting our feet on the table was certainly not the conduct expected from employees who would be representing British European Airways, whether on or off any of its sites.

I was thrilled. This was the opportunity I had been looking for to help my family. I gave Mom-mi and Dad-di the first of many free flights and upgrades I received, along with some of my other family members and friends. Mom-mi flew by Concorde to Jamaica and still talks about it to this day; also the time when I had to fly back from one of our holidays before them and they had to struggle through the airports to get home again. Never before had I earned so much money or was able to make sure that all of my siblings received a cash gift from me, a great trip, meal or support in some way. I always saved some of my salary so that I could carry on giving money and gifts to them. It was an amazing job. I think I must have visited every country in the world ranging from the Wailing Wall of Old Jerusalem to Buffalo, Las Vegas, Bethlehem and Chicago. Whether it was a long haul or short flight, whoever wanted to come with me did. My life became a whirl of cocktail bars, the gay and lesbian scene in Soho, always studying, with upgraded accommodation and partying until late. I often didn't have time to sleep. I went straight into work then, and I never forgot to send money to Mom-mi and Dad-di each month to help them.

The bits and pieces I gave to my siblings over the years gradually turned into emotional support, following any number of different crises which occurred. Occasionally we would go shopping and I would visit them at university. Irrespective of this, I always seemed to be the one to contact them, to give them updates on my life, and it was never reciprocated. I realised after a while that schadenfreude had set in. They were actually taking pleasure in any misfortune which I suffered. If something good happened to me, none of my cousins or other family members were interested. Conversely if it was anything negative, all of the details were requested and our lines of communication became fluid. They would call me back then for further updates.

Usually, if things were good, I didn't hear from anyone, only Mom-mi, who used to say, "quarn lef dem." When I got into the habit of going home less, I always telephoned to introduce her to my friends and boyfriends, again before I slept with them. This was my standard approach to dating. I didn't sleep with anyone unless they had sat in the filth at home, experienced the stench, and saw exactly where I had come from. I knew by then that, if someone could love you at your worst, then they would genuinely love you at your very best. However, this didn't make me any less of a fool so far as Adam was concerned!

Chapter Ten

Money Doesn't Always Lead To Happiness

A few years later I was crouched in the corner of the room, with my nose bleeding and sweat dripping onto the carpet; I tried to cover my head. He was using my hair extensions to drag me like a dirty blanket as I flailed, tried to punch him back, kicked and cursed. My knees and elbows had been scratched and rubbed on the cut pile carpet we chose carefully on a very different day. I tried to hold onto my extensions as they lifted, tore and became scattered around the room. Unable to drag me any further, he kicked me repeatedly and pushed my face hard against the window. I couldn't move so he slammed my head on the glass patio doors and, with every bit of strength I had left, I broke free. Breathless and panting, I dialled nine nine nine for help.

World War Three had erupted this time because of a minor correction I made to something he said during a conversation with my friends. The punch in my face caught me off guard when I was clearing up afterwards and it knocked me to the floor. He moved quickly. His punches and kicks caused me to roll into the ball I had used trying to protect myself as a child. Although I was exhausted; in pain and suffering from shock, I managed to fight back. The cursing and swearing continued as the phone went flying under the table. I made a dive for it but when I leaned under it to speak to the person on the other end of the line, he pulled me backwards using my legs, slamming my face on the edge of the table as he did so. Fortunately I was able to grab the phone again to shout for help.

Adam became aware then that someone else could hear what he was doing and he stepped away from me unclenching his fist. I shouted at him above the sound of him swearing. "I am calling the police!" When they arrived a little later with an ambulance, I collapsed onto the floor in relief. Taking a deep breath, I surveyed my surroundings. The brand new Neal's furniture was upside down. I could see a blood stain along the patio door and felt the bald patches on my scalp. The blonde and brown extensions had created their own flight path pattern along the newly laid carpet.

Adam always presented himself in public as a gentleman. He was seemingly everyone's friend, and yet an animal to live with. I was seven months pregnant on that occasion with our second child when he beat me. I was so glad that our other daughter was staying with his parents for the night, quite ironically to let us spend some time alone together. I was taken to the hospital covered in blood whilst our neighbours, in their million pound mansions, had been given another opportunity to discuss one of our fights. Before leaving the house, I threw the iron at him. It narrowly missed his head and shattered the glass door. I climbed off the stretcher the paramedics had put me on in front of our nosey neighbours so that I could leave the car keys on the roof of his brand new Jaguar XK8 in the driveway. I also succeeded in smearing the blood from my vagina onto its blue metallic paint before I limped back to the stretcher.

I had become so tired of my life with him, trying to pretend that everything was okay, hiding as much as I could from my daughter Laura whilst his punches and kicks made me curl into a ball crying, and wait for him to lose interest in what he was doing to me. I would slowly unwind myself from this position when I thought he was done. Although I was bruised and in pain, I had learned to make his tea afterwards and give him a cigar just as if nothing had happened. The bruises didn't show on my black skin but he was still a monster to live with. Doing as I was told, he enjoyed me urinating into his mouth every morning. Can you imagine what that was like, straddling him every day while he kept my urine soaked pants in his pocket. I learned later that he did this as a means of controlling me. By the time our marriage ended, I had a toddler and a five day old baby whom I had called Kay. One of the things which hurt the most was that my family still loved him. Before we married he would often turn up at the house to have tea with them. Just like me at the beginning, they couldn't see the wrong in anything he did.

However, that day proved to be the end of me being a millionaire's wife. My face was battered and my clothes torn. I couldn't walk properly so I hopped to the garage, covered in sweat and blood. There were bruises on my face, knees and hands. When I was lying on the stretcher outside, the paramedics and my neighbours just stared at me, not saying anything. I tried to wipe the blood away with a cloth, and I didn't cry. I decided then that I would never again live by another man's hand, but that meant becoming a single parent. The hostel was exactly as I thought it would be but it was the only place I could go. I used to pay for everything I bought with the cash Adam gave to me. I didn't have a credit card I could use. Whilst all the money I earned earlier had been absorbed into our marriage and my own house sold, I had also lost my self esteem and confidence. The other parents in the hostel stared at me. I was wearing a hospital gown, that was all. Nevertheless I didn't feel ashamed in asking for help but the thought of explaining to my family what had happened simply wasn't an option. They wouldn't understand.

"Yu do wha! Yu lef im? But wait... im nice man." I imagined them saying this. Even if I had been left for dead in our bedroom. The reality would be quite simple for them... 'Yu had it all, and yu left him!'

My mother also didn't understand that there really wasn't a choice, if I was going to survive. *Something had to change.* I guess that all of us have our demons to overcome and Adam had plenty of these. He was a young child when his mother died and he had been brought up by a succession of nubile nannies. His father was more interested in them than his son. I believe that he never learned the meaning of love, only what money could buy, including any woman he wanted, like me when I replaced his second wife, and the fourth one who came along shortly after I left.

I didn't know it at the time but I was about to enter some of the most difficult and confusing years of my life. Even more so than what I had already gone through. My father whom I dearly loved would pass away, without me being with him, and my mother was about to show me her beautiful heart. She had also changed over the years despite the pain she was going through from losing the man she had loved for most of her life, the one who had been her rock, she didn't fail me. She was at my side when I needed her the most, sharing every script and detail with my siblings, who never had to ask me anything, or share their concern as mom gave them minute detail, in which it would trickle out like a ripple of layers to whom they see fit.

Chapter Eleven

Ill Health Became A Part Of My Life

It started as a normal day. I had been looking forward to sitting with the girls as we usually did, to watch 'The Real Housewives Of Atlanta' at nine o'clock in the evening. I loved that show, and those women. I had taken off my bra, to make myself more comfortable in front of the television set. As I ran my hand under my armpit, stroking and cupping my breasts, I found a two centimetre area on the right hand side which didn't feel quite right. Exploring it further, I could tell that I definitely had a lump. Only a small one, the size of a pea, but I wasn't entirely sure whether it should be there. I played with it for a little longer, stroking and prodding it. Hell, I even squeezed it! I wasn't afraid. I didn't know then what that tiny lump would lead to, and I didn't want to miss the start of the show.

I played with it again when I remembered it was there. Perhaps I should have known better? Twenty years earlier, I had found a similar lump, and paid privately to have surgery to remove it. I had a breast augmentation not long afterwards; that was meant to be a treat. Once the decree absolute in my divorce from Adam had been sealed by the Court, I felt I deserved it. Given how acrimonious he had been, and made everything much worse than it needed to be, I didn't want anything from him, except enough money to look after the children properly. He kept the matrimonial home but obtaining regular child maintenance was a circus of allegations, litigation, accusations and wasted time and money for myself.

It used to make me think of the bible quote I read in 1 Corinthians, and how true it was. That all of us should be on guard against greed. Real life isn't about how many possessions we have, nor does money by itself lead to happiness. Adam caused a lot of trouble after I left him. At one point I was about to apply for an injunction to stop him from coming anywhere near us, when his new fiancee persuaded him to go on holiday with her. Not long after they came back, she moved into the house where the children and I had lived with him. As time went by it became very difficult to accept his plea of dire financial circumstances in the ancillary relief proceedings.

I eventually decided that the best option would be for me to try to put myself back into the position I was in before my marriage. Having given it a lot of thought, I decided to start studying again at night for a Masters degree in Law, and work as an educational consultant during the day. When I was at University I had been invited to attend a formal dinner in one of the Inns of Court in London. I wasn't sure at the time whether I would like the formality and ritual associated with this, but I did, so much so that it became something which stayed with me, and I wanted more of it. I didn't tell anyone else my secret wish. Nor did I realise that my world was going to be turned upside down again, and this time it would be because of ill health. Looking back now, I can see that God took me on the most amazing life journey; through the jobs and voluntary work I did, I was able to advise others and help them with their employment disputes. Also to give advice and guidance on housing and divorce. I volunteered in church for holiday summer camps, a prison ministry, and I became an approved foster carer for troubled teenagers when they needed an emergency short placement.

By the time I became aware that I had another lump in my breast, the girls and I were living in a beautiful house. However, as my health deteriorated, I couldn't carry on working to pay the mortgage. I found myself having long telephone conversations with the bank, trying to explain why I hadn't paid it for months, but I would magically be able to settle all of the arrears once it was sold. Our house had all the trappings of material wealth, 5 bedrooms and a loft conversion, with the benefit of ensuite bathrooms, a huge granite kitchen and Mediterranean tiles which still reminded me of the red geraniums in terracotta pots I loved when I had gone back to Italy after my divorce. It also had marble fireplaces, a charcoal log burner and underfloor heating. The furniture was sumptuous throughout, and I had more gadgets than I could possibly use in an entire lifetime. The parking area was large enough for five cars. Top of the range, of course, whilst the garden backed onto rolling hills and the wonderful English countryside.

My house and its grounds could easily have been featured in one of the glossy magazines I loved to read. I didn't want to leave but it was inevitable. I felt exhausted from the moment I opened my eyes in the morning until I closed them again at night. During my last conversation with the bank, I listened to the softly spoken cashier in the debt recovery department reminding me of the exact amount I owed. Telling me too that the next phase in the recovery process would start within days if I couldn't make a payment immediately. This meant that the house which had become my home, after leaving Adam was hanging by a thread, and it seemed certain I would lose it.

I was still waiting for the Department of Work and Pensions to make a decision on whether I was entitled to receive the interest on my mortgage from them, which I could transfer to the bank. If so, these payments could start twelve weeks after the date of my claim. I had been trying to sell the house for three years but not a single person had asked to view it. A new estate was being built nearby and this deterred prospective buyers. I had prayed every day and asked God to send me a buyer, all to no avail. I felt too ashamed to ask my family for help. I also didn't want to give some of them the opportunity of taking pleasure in my misfortune. I most definitely wasn't in the mood to play any more games.

My solicitor had advised me to go back to work but I couldn't do it. I wasn't well enough; I no longer had the energy. Apart from the lump, feeling continually ashamed and embarrassed by the change in my circumstances had contributed to a deterioration in my general health, especially when I learned that the debt recovery officer had not experienced anything like my situation in the whole of her career. It had become a Catch 22. Without a salary coming in, I also couldn't afford to pay the shortfall the bank was demanding, even if the interest only payments were made by the Government.

A few days later I finally applied for social housing because I didn't know what else to do. I didn't believe that there was anyone in my family I could turn to, and we had to live somewhere. I didn't have enough money to buy a smaller house or even pay the rent on one. Neither my parents nor anyone else I was related to had claimed state benefits in the past, certainly not lived in social housing, but I was desperate. After I made the application, any pride I had left was soon gone. I took my antidepressant tablets, a couple of sleeping pills, and I slept. On the outside I might still have been beautifully suited, and booted with manicured nails, pristine hair and make-up. Driving a traditionally grey Land Rover gave the illusion of wealth and glamour but on the inside I was broken, hurt and felt poorer than a stray dog. However, I was good at hiding my feelings, escaping into reality television, or sleeping all day. Either way was fine by me.

But things move on, as they must. Once I mentioned the lump in my breast to my General Practitioner, he didn't waste any time in sending me to the Priory Hospital locally. My cancer journey began in a variety of medical departments and waiting rooms. An hour before the mammogram I was booked in to undergo, I looked at the iPhone I had bought. The instructions on how to use it were clear enough. There was also some printed information I could read if necessary, and several well thought out images of what using the phone properly would look like. All of which led to the most conversations I had with my children in years. They would say things like, "Are you purchasing it yet? Show the picture to the man in the shop, so that he can see what's wrong. Make sure there is enough memory space. Don't charge, or open it!" The list of advice I received was endless. Given that they were both at school, I was shocked by the dedication and time they contributed to knowing every microscopic detail about my purchase of that phone while I was continually worrying about debt management and the bailiffs appearing at our front door, not least what to give them for tea. I shook my head in disbelief, wondering for the umpteenth time how I had actually managed to scrimp, save and go without other things, just so we could all have the latest mobile phones.

I checked my watch, meandered back to my car, and set off on the thirty minute drive to the Hospital. I found a parking space at two fifty-five and switched off the phone before strolling inside. I bought a coffee as I walked along the corridor to the x-ray department. I was careful not to spill it while I waited in the queue to confirm that I was there for the appointment. My hand felt as if it was burning from the heat of the plastic cup as I grabbed the hospital gown from the nurse with my other one. After I had put it on, I pushed my own clothes into the plastic bag she had also given to me, and sat down on one of the colourful chairs in the waiting area. Without thinking about what the mammogram might reveal, or the impact it could have on my life, I slurped the coffee, thankful that it was still hot, and switched the phone on again. Ignoring the numerous calls and texts I had received, I started to play Candy Crush.

'Jane Campbell,' a too young nurse announced before ushering me into a cold room which was white and pristine with a deadly looking machine inside it. My weight was checked and the procedure I was about to undergo explained to me. "Please remove your top and step onto the markers," she said, without any feeling in her voice.

Even though my breasts were about to be x-rayed, I was still worrying about my coffee. I had left it on her desk before standing on the markers, with my left hand placed strategically on the machine as instructed. My breasts were compressed and flattened onto a glass plate. When the nurse flattened each of them in turn, I winced, moaned, then cried out in pain. I could tell that she was looking at me disapprovingly so I tried to explain why what she was doing hurt so much. I reminded her that I had breast implants, only to be told that she was aware of this, and we carried on. I did my best to breathe deeply then sigh when she told me to. I held onto the machine firmly during the final compression, and tried to create a diversion for myself by wondering if I could get to level fifteen on Candy Crush.

At that critical point, the casual chatter between the doctor and nurse came to an abrupt halt. I felt a distinct shift in the atmosphere when they looked over the screen at each other. I was asked to get dressed, and come back to see the doctor in twenty minutes. When I had finished, I glanced in the changing room mirror, and held my breasts as if they were guns. Then I stared behind at my flat backside. Thinking I didn't look too bad, I finished what was left of the coffee, and walked along the corridor to the restaurant. I bought two of the latest magazines before going back to the waiting room at four o'clock. It was almost empty and I began to worry. It was time for the children to leave school and make their way home; they would be hungry, although there wasn't anything I could do about it, I checked the time again, flicked through the magazines and carried on playing Candy Crush, still fully intending to get to the next level.

The nurse eventually came out to see me, and was very friendly when she led me into a small room similar to a cupboard. It had prostheses, bras and a tiny couch inside. I noticed the badge she wore which said that her name was Mandy. I finally realised I was about to hear bad news. The doctor and her had the same look on their faces as they did before I went to the restaurant. I managed to laugh when I said, "Don't be giving me bad news!" Both of them looked down at the floor while the doctor told me the diagnosis. I only heard one word: Cancer! Everything else was muffled, like background noise. Petrified, and speechless by this time, I watched their lips move until I heard the next words: *Dead in six months...* and I shot out of the room.

Chapter Twelve

Telling My Children I Was Going To Die

It was raining heavily when I reached the car park. The blue skies and sunshine were gone. I tried to find my car, wandering backwards and forwards along the same path, but I felt too confused to see it. I had cancer? They had to be kidding me! I repeated this to myself in disbelief. Finally taking a deep breath, I found it. I slowly put on my seat belt and hesitated. Cancer, flipping heck. As the barrier lifted to let me out of the car park, tears were streaming down my face like the raindrops hitting the windscreen, they didn't stop. Anger swelled up inside me when the car behind bumped into mine. I didn't often get upset. I used to tell people to drive slowly and be careful instead of going too fast which could cause problems, but not that day. I sprang out of my car, forgetting about the rain, my tears, and how upset I was. Before I realised what I was doing, I was shouting at the driver of the vehicle behind mine. "Likkle pissing tail pickney, lik off me car!' The patois I had often heard, and spoken as a child, came back to my lips without a second thought.

The man seemed flustered by my outburst and he apologised whilst telling me that he couldn't avoid the collision. My car had rolled back into his.

I side eyed him, pulled up my lips, and cussed, "You liar, jan crow dog!" After a little more of this which was clearly going nowhere, we exchanged addresses and I quickly drove away, understandably not feeling any better about the news I had received.

The journey home became a blur. When I reached the house the girls had turned on the central heating and lit the fire to make it cosy. They were lying comfortably, side by side on the rug. As I walked in, I almost fell over their shoes and coats on the hall carpet, with the drawings they did at school, and plates of left over rice and curried chicken which had also been discarded. They came running after me into the kitchen, chattering about their day, they pushed important letters into my hands. They were happy to be home and see me again.

I could feel my heart swelling as I walked quietly into the living room and sat down. The girls followed me, looking pointedly at each other, wondering what was going on. I took a deep breath. Noticing how hot it was and that they had put even more envelopes and letters on the stairs for me to deal with, I didn't stop to think. I blurted out that I only had six months to live. I had cancer. I will never forget that moment. The three of us, holding each other and crying. I realised that I had made a mistake in how I told them. I had done it too quickly, without any preparation. I vowed that this would be the last time I cried because of my illness but I didn't know that life was about to get a whole lot worse.

Less than an hour after telling my daughters that I had cancer, I broke the news to my sister Juliet. When I put the phone down, I tried to cheer the kids up by watching television with them. Three hours later, every single member of my family was sitting in my house. It was very cold and any thoughts I had about pulling myself together soon disappeared. As I was walking through the hall, I could overhear their conversation. Juliet was saying quite clearly, "She has lost everything this time! Her home, job and health. But that's only the beginning!" From the tone in her voice, I could tell that she believed I had brought this sorry state of affairs on myself.

I stumbled over the shoes and bags which they had discarded before walking into the kitchen across the Italian tiles I loved. Even though the marble was cold, I knelt down in front of them to pray, and I asked God to give me the strength to get through this. I hadn't been given the luxury of breaking the news to the members of my family one at a time since all of them felt it was their duty to inform the others as soon as they heard what had happened to me, using the different means at their disposal, calling, texting or messaging on social media. It didn't get any better. As soon as they knew about my cancer, it became general chit chat and the beginning of most of their conversations. I became the subject of whispers or side long glances. How far I had fallen was the best local, national and international news they had heard in a long time, whilst all I felt inside was despair and an emptiness which was growing stronger every day.

My cancer treatment started with another bang. I had ultrasound treatment, a biopsy, bone scan, CT scan and an xray of my pelvis in quick succession. A letter had also arrived giving me a date for the mastectomy. This clashed with the Hearing date I already had for an application I was making to the Employment Tribunal. It had taken me nearly two years of hard work to get everything ready for the Hearing. The long nights I spent transcribing conversations I had recorded, considering how best to challenge my former employer on the company's minutes, witness statements and legal arguments. The countless hours talking to my former colleagues who had either won or entered into compromise agreements with our former employer, gave me the motivation I needed to carry on. I spent hours after work or at night classes, after the children were in bed, preparing my case for this five day hearing, whilst also getting the legal training I needed to apply for a pupillage and become a trainee Barrister, only to discover that this would be on the same day as I was due to have a mastectomy operation. No! It must be a mistake.

Not only that, I had also attended a cognitive behavioural therapy group for twelve weeks, trying to cope with my obsessive compulsive disorder which had again been triggered by stress, anxiety, and depression. Unable to sleep, while I prepared for my employment tribunal Hearing that would last five days, had been awful. Papers littered the floor in neat bundles, with colour coded post it notes all in date order, extended along the hall and up the stairs. I was hunched over them morning until night, opening each bundle, flicking through every single scenario, trying to put them in chronological order.

The printer was working nonstop whilst black plastic folders were strewn across the floor. The children's ballet lessons came in handy; they could pirouette through them on tip toes to go to the bathroom.

I lived without sleep and this meant being on a constant merry go round of worry in which, if I even saw the outline of the ivy plant, it freaked me out. It was bizarre! Green, silky, webbed ivy crawling up the wall would leave me itching for hours afterwards and shrugging my shoulders. The endless cleaning and wiping continued. I couldn't cope with clutter, dust or untidy surfaces. Felix the cat had to wear slippers. He was not allowed to run around on his bare paws inside the house. He would patiently wait on the carpet until I had wiped each paw and sprayed them before entering his given area. He lived in the hall because I was unable to cope. The therapist I was seeing felt that the new job I had by this time found, and planning for the tribunal, had simply been too much.

My Solicitor thought that there would be time for the Tribunal to hear all the evidence I had collated. Three trolley suitcases full of the paperwork, the illicit tape recording I had taken of an important meeting, and the minutes my employer had subsequently sent out which differed significantly from it. I was exactly like a child in the way I had an urgent need for my case to be heard. I wanted them to pay for what they had done to me, and to hear their excuses why the minutes did not match my recording. I dreamed of having my day in court, getting more compensation, and at the very least recovering the fees I had paid to my Solicitor. I was confident that she had the ability to win. She had a lot of experience in employment law and had successfully presented many cases at the Tribunal.

Everything was prepared. We were ready to go! The documents had been indexed in chronological order before being put into box files. Copies of the tape recording could be provided if this was challenged so, getting the twenty-fifth November as a hearing date and being booked in for a mastectomy operation at the same time, was a complete disaster. My thoughts constantly twisted and turned. Everywhere I looked I couldn't find any peace. I thought about committing suicide. Stress, depression and the loneliness of it all had by this time set in. I was living on autopilot, not communicating with anyone. Prayer sometimes offered me a little comfort but I still felt empty inside. Suicide looked like the best option and I couldn't stop thinking about it. The thought lingered, whispering softly to me, so much so that I started to find it comforting. I began to listen. I was drowning and no one realised it. That particular day its whisper had become louder, somehow connecting deeper within me.

I decided that I could do it when the children were at school. I didn't care anymore about having cancer, the bills I needed to pay, my mortgage, earning a living, nothing. All I wanted was to be gone from this world, and I intended to be. The only problem was, I didn't want my daughters to find me afterwards, which meant I had to arrange for them to be picked up from school. *Where was God in my darkest hour? I felt completely alone.*

The following morning, I couldn't get them out of the house fast enough. I told them everything was going to be okay. I held them tightly, smelt the soap on their clean skin, and watched them getting ready to go to school, eating their breakfast, chattering, and eventually getting into the taxi I had booked. As soon as they left, I slammed the front door and ran up the stairs faster than Usain Bolt. Without giving myself time to think about what I was doing, I grabbed all of my Sertraline anti-depressant tablets. I even looked on the floor to make sure I hadn't missed any because I intended to take every single tablet in the house. I reached the point when I didn't care what it was. Hunger came and went. I was focusing by then on the paracetamol tablets I had found. As I ripped the foil packaging, and put them into a supermarket carrier bag with the rest of my medication, I sat on the edge of my bed, determined that today would be my last one.

I found it too difficult to contact the Chambers and withdraw my application for the job they had offered to me. I was hurting too much, my body ached, I felt heavy, and useless. I didn't have a choice, I wanted out! I was reaching inside the bag to grab my first handful of pills when I noticed a yellow sticky note on the outside of it. Someone had telephoned and left a message for me. I had been asked to go back to the hospital for a full body scan. There was a problem with my blood. It was urgent that I do this. The word today had been underlined. The message slipped from between my fingers onto the ground. I couldn't take this anymore. I didn't even have the energy to cry. A huge, grey, fog had been following me for a long time. The despair and depression I felt was overwhelming. I couldn't cope. I had lost the ability to make the simplest of decisions, By now I was completely exhausted and felt nauseous. I put my hand inside the plastic bag again to grab a handful of pills. I looked at them. They were small, white and mostly Sertraline or Gabapentin. As I slowly lifted my hand to put the tablets into my mouth, my mobile phone rang.

    I wanted to scream that I was busy. I intended to kill myself. I had cleaned the house and the children had been given clear instructions about who would be picking them up after school. I really was about to do it. Irrespective of this, the phone carried on ringing. If it was me making the call I would have given up; It was perfectly clear that I wasn't going to answer. I eventually stopped what I was doing, with the tablets in my hand, and walked slowly onto the landing. Why had the person on the other end of the call not given up but was still waiting for me? When I did answer the phone all I heard was, "Hello! *God loves you.*" No introduction or formalities, just that, but it was enough. I collapsed onto the floor so that I could kneel and pray. I had believed for a long time that Angels exist to stop us from doing something which we are not meant to.

Chapter Thirteen

The Lord Reached Out To Me

It seemed perfectly clear to me that day, God had reached out to me. I left the house and went to the hospital as quickly as I could. The same nurse I had seen earlier greeted me and told me about her four year cancer journey. She described the treatment she received and warned me I would need to fight the illness, that I couldn't give up. I sat and listened to her, feeling exhausted and depressed. My only relationship with the hospital before my cancer journey began had taken place many years earlier. When I was sixteen years old, I washed the pots for nine months and filled the patient trays until my application came through for the army. The hospital was now going to become my home. Within thirty minutes of my arrival, I had been given eight appointments over the following ten days. I was to undergo a full body scan; a number of blood tests, an endoscopy, sigmoidoscopy, chest and body x-rays, not forgetting an immediate blood transfusion, followed by deep thrombosis anti-coagulation visits, and a lot more. The big one would be meeting my oncologist for chemotherapy treatment.

At the time I didn't know that my mother would be with me throughout this stage in my life. "Rahted soup, a wha dis?" she had asked when I was formally diagnosed as having oestrogen receptive breast cancer. No one had given me any actual details about the mastectomy, chemotherapy or radiation I would need; that all of it would last a long time during which I would need to learn how to manage the pain and the side effects whilst also trying to absorb the long term cost of everything. Equally I didn't have anything to say or contribute if I was asked a question by the doctors. When the pain licked me, I went to them to fix it. As far as I was concerned, reality was on hold and everything I did seemed to be automatic. I didn't have any words to describe the endless round of appointments and waiting time in between them. At every appointment, I attended I didn't say a word. I simply focused on the faces in front of me, how the doctors and nurses looked when they read my results. I didn't have the energy to speak. I felt like a lump of lard that was melting away, and I still very much wanted out.

Nevertheless, human kindness exists in the most unlikely of places. I found it in the strangers I met briefly who were at varying stages in their own cancer journeys. They shared their experiences with me as we sat twiddling our thumbs in hospital chairs, waiting for it to be our turn to be seen. This certainly wasn't the life I had in mind for myself years ago when I made all those plans with Angelica. I was supposed to be on top by this time, at the start of my new career, sitting in an office as a trainee Barrister. If everything had gone according to my earlier life plan, I might even have been able to tell the bank that I could make the payments they wanted, and not let my house slip away. I also wouldn't have had to complete their debt recovery forms, or bankruptcy papers.

Lord, you have helped me overcome poverty in the past! I endured sexual abuse, fought ancillary relief proceedings for my children, and was homeless. Yet you also gave me those beautiful girls, Laura and Kay, then allowed me to do everything for them. The marriage I went through, and the debts which came afterwards, during which most of my own family scorned and ignored me until they decided to completely exclude me from their lives. It reached the point where all they had was contempt for me when I was diagnosed as suffering from cancer.

"Give me strength, Lord!" the frightened girl within me said quietly, as I sat on the hospital chair that day and stared straight ahead. I knew my face must be expressionless and blank simply because I no longer had anything left to give to life, or could comment on. That's who I had become. The middle of my back was on fire, the lower back pain was unbearable. Even my feaces had gone from a green tinged yellow to red. I could no longer control my toilet habits. Midway through a conversation, it wasn't unusual for me to run to the nearest one. I had almost crawled into the Directions Hearing at the employment tribunal twelve months ago, representing a client - and the Judge allowed me to lean over a chair for comfort. It must have been a strange sight but I was very grateful to him. Doing this gave me some relief from the pain when my back had become rigid, as it had done that day. I had suffered from constant middle back ache and headaches for almost a year by then. All of it was beginning to make sense. The stress, and worry, along with those endless days in bed, shortness of breath, loss of appetite, constipation and piles in one week, followed by diarrhoea the next. Perhaps more importantly, the chest pains I had which were left undiagnosed? *God had taken me into the wilderness.* Not to leave me there, alone and suffering, but so that I could change. He wanted to show me my true path in life.

Now my diary was full and I still had more to fit into it. I was broke too. I no longer had the petrol money to use my car so that I could get to the appointments and home again. The realisation hit me that I would have to walk. My first chemotherapy appointment was at eight thirty in the morning. I arrived fifteen minutes early and sat down to wait. I counted twenty-eight bright pink chairs in the room. They were soft and sturdy with heavy legs. There were some magazines to read but the Wi-Fi didn't work. I heard the receptionist mention it to a colleague and they carried on complaining about this while I waited. The waiting room was warm which felt good. My heating bills for the previous year had been nearly three thousand pounds since I always felt cold, regardless of the weather.

Slowly and surely, the other patients began to arrive, asking questions which I couldn't quite hear. The early signs of cancer began to reveal themselves as I reflected on what had happened to me up to that point. I felt scared and unhappy in that bright and beautifully decorated waiting room. It had a cheerful notice board with cuttings attached to it, snippets of information about the staff and hospital, the names of the people who worked there, their roles, and who had been given the accolade of nurse of the week. I felt nauseous and my middle back was rigid. I know I must have looked awkward. My mouth was also hanging down like a wet fish. Okay, I was totally pissed off! I couldn't even be bothered replying to the nurses, patients or the doctor. The pain had overwhelmed me so much so that I was feeling confused again, and totally bewildered, like a deer trapped in the headlights.

When the nurse introduced herself, she began the speech she had learned, by telling me that I didn't have to say anything. I looked down when she said this, I didn't care about any of it. I wanted to scream and tell her that she needed to do what she had to, then let me go. I walked into the treatment room to be met by the ubiquitous chairs which were on this occasion in a box position. They were fluorescent pink, also orange and green, the effect resembled an old folk's home. People sat on them reading magazines and cards, music was bopping around in the background, tea, coffee, and other refreshments were available. The patients seemed to be at different stages in their recovery. It was a mixed age group and a lot were older than me. Some had started casual conversations; they were even laughing, despite everyone in the room being attached intravenously to a drip. My heart sank. Welcome to chemotherapy, I couldn't help thinking to myself!

A nurse was about to insert a needle into my vein for the chemotherapy FEC-T when I screamed and fainted. It was the final straw, I loathed needles. I awoke in one of the patient bays two hours later, with the feeling that I was going to be sick. When it was finally time for me to go home, I received a huge bag of medication to take with me. I don't know how I managed to get home or what I was supposed to do with all of the tablets in the bag, and injections I had to administer myself. I hadn't listened when they told me what I would need to do, but at least my bed and mattress were my friends. I had been given Dexamethasone, a corticosteroid which prevents the release of substances causing inflammation. I also had Domperidone, a dopamine antagonist, and Filgrastim injections for my low white blood cells. The silver needles I had to insert into my stomach were long and sharp, apparently failsafe. The anticoagulation medication was also in the bag because I had been wearing the tightest pop socks I could buy whilst the Aprepitant tablets had been prescribed for my endless nausea and vomiting.

After looking at all of this for a minute or two, I ran the tap to swirl the water and tablets down the plug hole. I had a headache, I was shivering and always seemed to be retching. It wasn't long before I went back to sleep, with Mom-mi and my children staring down at me. I felt boiled, cooked and mashed by all this. All the days and nights began to merge into each other. I had an urge to push and the blood from my period erupted uncontrollably onto the bed. I drifted in and out of consciousness while my children and Mom-mi changed my bed sheets, or scurried around me, until I was no longer wet but in a hospital gown. My head, hands and feet had become heavy with pins and needles; I couldn't do this anymore, I really couldn't! My other worries had paled into insignificance. All I wanted was to be pain free. I still had another eight chemotherapy sessions to get through, with the endless monitoring and appointments to attend.

Mom-mi eventually called an ambulance. My left leg had gone and I couldn't breathe. My daughters, who were in the middle of their GCSE courses, were crying. I knew that they were having to do far too much, and see more than they should. "God give me strength!" They deserved a medal for the help they gave me when I was ill whilst the oncologist had mapped out my life for the next two years. Eight rounds of FEC-T were in my diary, and I was to have Docetaxel chemotherapy sessions every twenty-one days. Whether I would need a bilateral mastectomy ten months later wasn't clear at first, but the doctor told me that the implant had burst in my cancerous breast so this one had to be removed. I could look forward to Herceptin injections every twenty-one days for eighteen months afterwards because of it. Following the chemotherapy, I would have radiation every day for six weeks, with separate hospital appointments six months after the mastectomy. Perhaps it had been a kindness when no one told me about the side effects, delays or countless nights when I would need to call an ambulance, usually because of the worsening problems with my back, leg and breathing, or the mini strokes I had which delayed the procedures already booked into my diary.

I couldn't control what was happening. Everything was out of order now, and the memories I had were confused. It said on the oncology plan we made at the start, that I would have a mastectomy after eight treatment sessions of chemotherapy at twenty-one day intervals. Instead, the procedure had been intermittent because of my breathing difficulties, blood clots on my lungs, and I also had a stroke. This had delayed the timetable by almost sixteen months. The most frightening side effect had been the loss of memory I suffered; I was unable to recall even the smallest of details, or concentrate on anything.

When I awoke from the operation, my daughters were at the hospital with Mom-mi and Juliet. Lord have mercy! I was still alive, but in so much pain. I was surprised to be hungry too. I only had one breast, and I needed to use the toilet. My entire torso was pinned to the bed. I was in excruciating pain from the waist upwards. My entire neck down to my waist was frozen. I couldn't move, or speak. My body felt heavy as I laid flat on my back, covered in bandages. I overheard my daughters asking the doctor how long it would be before the bandages could be removed. One of the nurses had put a cardboard container underneath my bottom, but I knew that if I tried to urinate into it I would soak the bed. The doctor was still explaining the process to my family, telling them that the breast implant had burst, and had been successfully removed. My breast prosthesis in its transparent plastic container was being examined closely by them. While I lay there desperately wanting to scream.

God alone knows how my daughters coped with me being in hospital during that time. Juliet had travelled from Manchester to stay with them. She hadn't previously shown any interest in doing this. From the day they were born, I told her things about them, the parties they had, the plays they were in, and other school events. I also told her about my marriage and divorce, the holidays we had. She didn't show any interest whatsoever in any of this, or the girls' career choices, at one stage the possibility of them joining the profession she was in. I asked her repeatedly to let them visit her every summer but my words fell on deaf ears. She came to my home once when I bought it, preferring after that to see me at Mom-mi's house, and find out anything else she wanted to know from the telephone calls she had with Elsey. My world had been truly turned upside down.

Chapter Fourteen

Everything Began To Change Once I Had Faith

As I lay in the hospital bed, it dawned on me that I might not have been thinking about things in the right way. I hadn't been looking clearly at who or what I had become. What the hell was I thinking? The medication and pain had made me confused and forgetful for a long time. Wearing a loosely fitting night gown, I had awoken that morning in excruciating pain across the entire left side of my body; I could barely breathe, the rasping, and my shortness of breath felt surreal, as if my spirit was somehow in a parallel universe looking down on my broken body. I looked around the four bed ward in slow motion, taking in the pristine, shiny, tiles as the nurses moved quickly. I could tell that they were trying to tidy the ward and make it look as inviting as possible for the visitors. The three other patients in the beds near mine appeared to be glued to them, motionless, amid the faint beeping of heart monitors and low muffled voices.

   It was easy for me to groan inwardly, although I wasn't sure if it had actually made a sound. My neck was stiff and my chest felt tight as I breathed heavily, I couldn't move my left arm, it wasn't doing what I wanted it to; my left leg also felt heavy. There was a peculiar throbbing sensation moving up and down my left side. I was in so much pain that I couldn't decide what to do to try and ease it. Any attempt to shuffle or move only increased the agony. Even the tiniest shift exacerbated it. I could barely hear the voices coming from behind the washed out grey curtains diagonally opposite me. The smell of stale coffee and uneaten food hit my nostrils. I grimaced just as the curtain rail around my bed was thrown back abruptly and the footsteps I had heard shuffling across the floor reached me.

"A pulmonary embolism," the doctor was saying, as the nurse and a trainee doctor stared intently at the scars on my neck. I averted my eyes. When I tried to speak, dizziness and breathing difficulties overwhelmed me. I waved my right hand instead somewhere into the air as soon as I realised that I could still move it. Doctor Khan responded to this weak attempt at finding out more without looking at me properly. He explained automatically what was going to happen next while I tried my best to listen to him before the intensity of the pain overcame me again.

"You are suffering from shortness of breath, chest pain and chronic fatigue because of the blood clot inside your lungs. We are going to reschedule your oophorectomy so that we can examine it. The clot is presently restricting the flow of blood into your lungs and decreasing your oxygen levels," he said, clearly not expecting me to reply.

A large bubble of bright green mucus which had the appearance of otherworldly slime protruded from the side of my mouth, as I tried again to say what I wanted to. I flailed around in frustration on the bed, despite the pain I was in, distressed by the lack of control I had over what was happening to me. The nurse leaned down to capture the globule of mucus once it was dangling from my chin. She dealt with it in a single swoop and I pressed my body deeper into the soft mattress, emotionally, and physically exhausted. A pulmonary embolism? No Sir, that couldn't be right! I had tried to kill myself even though I couldn't remember exactly what had happened. Except for a poor attempt at swallowing crushed sertraline, paracetamol, gabapentin and anything else I could find, with death hovering around me.

My saving grace had been forgetting to close the back door, and that it was the children's half day at school because of a teacher training session. Just before they arrived home, I remembered this, but I had no idea of when it had actually happened. I crawled into the ensuite bathroom and put my fingers down my throat so that all of the tablets I had swallowed could spew into the toilet. I lay on the floor afterwards while my chest erupted like a volcano. I couldn't breathe, even after I heard the children's feet pounding up the stairs to share their day with me. I awoke in hospital later on.

A lot of things seem strange looking back at this time. I am still not sure that I have recalled everything in the right order. I also discovered that people react differently when they find out someone has cancer. You might think that I should have known better by then; three months into the long periods I spent waiting for treatment made me question who I was. Why all of this should have happened to me. These enforced episodes of isolation, calm and quietness gave me time to reflect. It wasn't possible to place a value on the days I spent in a side ward, or at home alone back then. Whilst the ups and downs of everyday life continued for others, I was given the opportunity to analyse my life, what had happened in the past and the people in it. The importance of life itself, God's grace, and the mercy which He had shown to me, helping me get to the point which I had reached.

Ultimately, everything which had happened to me caused me to reaffirm my commitment to God, to give Him my pledge that I would pray and be thankful every day in the future. If anything compromised my peace it had to go, including people. I was unable to cope with stress, so didn't have any choice. The more I thought about this, I believed that I could rely on God to deal with all of it, provided I honoured my commitment to Him. Of course, I still made mistakes. I wasn't perfect but my focus gradually became clearer, asking questions like who, what, where, when and how much, meant absolutely nothing to me. I had to be stripped back emotionally, financially and physically before I could see the true gift of life itself, to find a spiritual relationship which brought me peace, and the realisation that good health was vitally important. All the years I had wasted when I didn't know this, or understand. No amount of physical fitness, a high end work place, or social status, big house and car, alcohol or drugs, could exceed a simple act of kindness. The value of respect and making time for others, a hug, smile or kiss, listening to someone speak and the touch of warmth, impressed me more at that time than anything else in my entire journey. Even though I spent a lot of time alone with my thoughts, I was finally able to see this.

And the result of all this reflection? I eventually came to believe cancer was the best thing that had happened to me. It had revealed the best and the worst in humanity. It clarified who was prepared to give and offer me support instead of schadenfreude. However, I am grateful to everyone for the part they played in my journey and healing. Isaiah 26 verse 3 tells us that God will keep us in perfect peace if our minds stay focused on Him. Deciding to fully commit to Him, lean on Him and trust Him to be the centre of my life, had surprising results. Instead of focusing on myself as I had been doing, everything began to change. I also won my tribunal case and was baptised for the second time.

Chapter Fifteen

God Sends The Hardest Battles So We Can Heal

While I was still lying in a hospital bed, I remember walking around the village where we lived. Perhaps it was only a dream? All that country air, the sound of the brook gushing forth, young families on their bicycles, people having picnics in the park, and I was enjoying myself. My daughters were fourteen and sixteen years old. They kept me on my toes, loved gadgets and were clearly academics; mostly awkward and rude, in small doses, they were fantastic. Even if they did sometimes run me ragged, I kept my eyes closed, praying to God to give me strength and help me go back to sleep with more of this wonderful memory. During my third chemotherapy session, the hair on my body began to gently fall away. It was too late now to think about putting the top sheet on the bed, something I usually did so that I could remove the hairs more easily. I was too tired to move... I was drowning and no-one else could see me doing it.

    I didn't know what God was doing at first. I couldn't see it or that He was the light shining in the darkness. I simply believed that my life was awful. I was alone in my suffering. I didn't realise that, by having faith in Him, this could truly change everything. I hadn't heard of the poem by William Cowper, written years ago, which became a hymn about God moving in a mysterious way. Having cancer gave Him the opportunity to sort the chaff from the wheat. It felt as if He had crushed me like corn, between two heavy grindstones, stripping me back financially, emotionally and physically until I was like dust. At the same time He was opening me up spiritually as I recovered in my own patch of wilderness. During this lonely and confusing time, my thoughts had been filled with negativity. I thought about the impact my earlier behaviour had on others and their attitude towards me during my illness; all those who had turned their backs when I needed help, many of whom were members of my family, causing me to place my trust completely in God. He had, by this time, brought me through so much. All of the main events in my life, including the betrayals I suffered, evil plotting of my enemies, their schadenfreude attitude and behaviour towards me, which had hurt me badly.

Looking back, these negative thoughts always seemed to appear when my health was at its worst, like when I had suffered a complete loss of feeling on my left side, with excruciating pain in my left leg and arms; or lying flat on my back because of the problems with my spine, and the fractures I suffered to both arms. I had tripped, slipped and fallen when I was feeling confused and anxious about my latest set of results. The long corridor of depression took hold of me, so much so that I lived inside its grey walls, under what seemed to be a ceiling made of fog. The pressure of the windows weighed me down even further. I could hear the doctors walking through the house in a robotic fashion, and see the mail piled up high waiting for me to attend to it, while all I could do was mumble inaudible sounds. Suicide sat demurely in the distance with its door ajar, sweetly whispering, "Come in! Come in!"

After a while, I realised that our circumstances don't need to be perfect for our lives to be a demonstration of God's love for us. I still believe to this day that it was part of His plan to leave me alone and broken. If He hadn't done this, I wouldn't have relied on reading my bible, the only way I had of gaining a clear understanding into what was happening to me while I spent hours waiting for doctors and surgery, unable to walk or barely move. During this time my trusted bible, its verses and prayer became my only source of connection. I realised that I hadn't read enough of my bible before I was taken ill. Prayers, praise and meditation have now become the cornerstones of everything I do; I have created routines around them. *From the moment my eyes open or when my feet touch the floor each morning, I say a simple "thank you, Lord." This leads me into prayer, and meditation.* As I suffer from insomnia, anytime and every time is for prayer, a simple exercise I can do around the house, in the shower or when I cook and clean. Every moment of my life gives me the opportunity to talk to or hear from God. He taught me this when I was ill.

I sometimes smile about it now. I feel as if I have turned into one of those elderly Jamaican women who share their experiences as they walk, and tell the world how God has given them salvation. Nothing shocks me any more, surprises or affects me. Since I started to truly believe in Him, I have fully accepted Lord Jesus Christ as my Saviour and King. It's all down to whether we choose carnality or a spiritual life. There isn't an in between place. The decision regarding the way we live is set by our heart and spirit.

Also, the importance of not being led astray, not being fooled by those Pastor pimps, Bishop's boppers and Missionary movers, or the higher than thou church brothers and sisters who spend more time choosing which outfit or shoes to wear before they attend a service. Their nails and hair are immaculate while they focus on who can talk the longest in the pulpit. Christians can be carnal too, nobodies off limits and materialistic, demanding the latest, newest and biggest items in the store; with an unforgiving, boastful, proud, lying and cheating, jealous, promiscuous, all about me nature, and self rules. Allowing carnality to take over our lives instead of overcoming the flesh, the world and its enemy through the authority and power of God. In the case of carnality, the flesh rules. The world has a hold on this person and the enemy gained an entrance.

We are in perilous times, everyone wants to be mean, high, badass, aloof, heroic, worshipped, sexy or downright rude. Running on the weak willed, superficial, power hungry, fashion conscious, materialistic, look at me attitude – where right is wrong and wrong is right.

I know from my own life that the Devil himself has a killer work ethic. He is consistent, and relentless in keeping carnal people close to him. The flesh is Satan's workshop, his preferred realm of operation. I am thankful to have learned now to overcome this through prayer in Jesus Name and put Satan out of work. Jehovah Adonai, the Sovereign Lord, can make all things work together for His good. There is no entrenchment of sin that has gone so far that the power of the Risen Lord, through his Holy Spirit, can't go further. During my illness, because of the pain I was in and the amount of medication I took, I often didn't know where I was. My thoughts used to take me into the past, rolling and tumbling through my head as I laid in my hospital bed, not realising at the time that this was happening. It was only later that I knew God had done this to protect me from what I could at times no longer bear.

"If she thinks I'm having dem kids, it ain't going so!" Juliet's words sounded like an animal barking, while I was lying on the same bed as when I was a child, my thoughts zoning in and out of the argument taking place around me.

"Me garn, not in the mood for this," Delroy said, by way of a gentle retaliation, and I allowed my ears to imagine what my eyes couldn't see. I heard the loud clash of crockery coming from the kitchen when the ceramic plates were taken out of the cupboard. Also the sound of bubbles rising to the top of the water in the pan, meat sizzling and the seasoning being shaken onto it. I knew that Mom-mi would be using the back of her forearm to wipe the sweat from her face as she slaved over the stove. I could almost taste the food we were going to eat that day. It was Saturday, so pea soup with boiled yam, green banana, dumplings and clumps of mutton on the bone. Who would have thought the memory of this meal and a family argument could be so comforting when I remembered it later? The conversation between my brother and sister had come to an abrupt halt presumably because Mom-mi had walked into the room. No words needed to be said. A single glance from her was comparable to a bolt of lightning, sufficient to shake the room. One dreadful flash, and there would be silence.

The flannel bed sheet brushed against my face, bringing me back to reality. The cold hard truth was an eye-opener! Not all the time and love we gave to others was going to be reciprocated, or even recognised by them, it didn't matter who we were. This would happen to all of us at some point in our lives. My hand gripped the soft blanket on the bed and I pulled it upwards under my nose. I inhaled deeply, attempting to use the aroma of the bed linen to take me back to my childhood and family, before a shooting pain ran up my spine, forcing me into the present. The pain can only be described as comparable to being grasped by the Devil himself, dragging me relentlessly downwards into the depths of hell. I was in my own bed, with only my memories to keep me company, and the isolation felt like a cold blanket. I knew that most people would, at some point in their lives, believe they had reached rock bottom. My time had finally come when I was abandoned by my family, had a failed marriage behind me, and was suffering from a life-threatening illness.

A tear slid down my cheek. After all this time I could still remember lying on Mom-mi's bed as a child, immersed in that glorious scent of roses and lavender. I closed my eyes again and tried to envision myself in the meadow, surrounded by beautiful flowers. Just as I began to drift into the daydream, a loud bang brought me back. The front door had slammed which meant Mom-mi was home. As I sprang out of bed like a Jack in the box, the sheets clung to my foot. My excitement quickly changed to humiliation and pain when my face hit the thinly carpeted floor. The world stopped turning while I decided whether to laugh or cry. I was a child again and a grazed knee could suddenly become the end of the world. Luckily, I saw the humour in my situation that day so I picked myself up and ran down the narrow staircase.

The colour of Elsey's skin fascinated me when I was a child, and hearing how the visitors to our house described it. "Let her sleep!" Mom-mi said, firmly when she saw me edging closer to the new baby. Other curious faces had been looking through the doorway at her from every corner of the house, all of them hoping to catch a glance of the new arrival, whilst here she was, my new baby sister looking so pretty, wearing a pink bonnet with a knitted cardigan that matched, happy and healthy, gurgling to herself and totally oblivious of her audience, a welcome addition to our family. At my young age and not realising how powerful words could be, I stepped closer to her and asked why her skin was so dark, simply repeating what I had heard several of the adults say. A few dagger-like glances were quickly thrown my way, but I carried on undeterred with the comment that she really was black!

"God gave us different shades, but we are all the same inside," Mom-mi said sternly, by way of explanation. Elsey was to be in later life the most beautiful person you could ever want to meet, physically and spiritually.

A loud clash came from the kitchen. Juliet was clearly washing up again. "Don't mash up me plate dem," Mom-mi bellowed down to her. Another spurt of venom erupted from her when my sister continued her assault on the crockery. The lingering anger from yet another argument with Delroy. "Juliet! Me won't tell you again," Mom-mi said, in an even louder voice whilst I watched the bundle of joy begin to examine the room. Dad-di's bright colours decorating the walls of our house. The bright, yellow, living room had an uplifting aura because of the fluorescence of the wallpaper. The cinnamon and green carpet was covered in crimson swirls. In the corner of the room I could see the gramophone record player, the side of which had been heavily decorated with doilies. A large glass fish was used as a centerpiece, with Mom's hair treasures behind it.

I looked back at my baby sister. "Come on! Do something." I said, bored by her inability to entertain me.

"What do you expect, Jane? What do you want her fi do?" Mom-mi said, raising her eyebrows. After thinking about it carefully, I decided that my best option would be to keep my smart remarks to myself so I simply shrugged my shoulders, pretending I didn't know the answer to her question.

"How about she packs your shit for you, and you leave?" Juliet shouted nastily from the kitchen. The rest of the family who were there began to laugh like a pack of wild hyenas, and Mom-mi stood up. "Don't think you are too old for the slipper,

Juliet," she replied, with a smirk on her face. The baby's gurgles attempted to dissipate this light hearted argument, and my Mother sighed when she sat down again. I pressed myself deeper into the couch, still wondering why and where this venom, nastiness came from. Juliet and Elsey were voluptuous, beautiful, had copious partners but none lasted long or were ever good enough. When I tried to sit up, a dull pain suddenly began to throb on one side of my brain. It became more powerful, as the Devil's hand reached into the depths of my childhood and threw me back to the present. A bittersweet feeling came over me. I remembered again the first time I had laid eyes on Elsey. The regrets I had later for constantly questioning, repeating her skin colour. The vibration of my mobile phone interrupted my thoughts. It was still on my bedside table and fully charged. Unplugging it, I escaped from this half-asleep world into playing a present day Candy Crush, and watching reality television.

Having cancer changed every single part of my life. The impact was huge, spiritually, physically, emotionally and financially. I believed that it would never end. It was only much later that I understood God sends the strongest battles for us to fight, to shape, mould and change us. Cancer had allowed the scum in my life to rise to the surface so that I could deal with it and heal. It taught me that good health outweighed everything else. This lesson became all too true when sorting myself out after using the toilet was almost too painful to do. I soon learned that having an expensive car in the garage wasn't any help with that!

It also revealed my Mother's beautiful soul in her consideration, and the time she dedicated to us. Everything she did for my daughters and I when I became too ill to look after myself was priceless. Yet this was the same woman who had been so cruel in her blind parenting across the sixties, seventies and eighties; the mistakes she had made back then with her own children. She had changed too across the years. When I became an adult, she was much more westernised. Having learned to speak calmly, and lovingly to me, our forty-seven year relationship tipped on its head to become one of love and warmth. Only a few cross words were spoken after that, with her ability to listen to all her visitors' woes and continually share.

All of this was very different to my teenage years. I had my first period when I was thirteen years old. I vividly remember walking into the bathroom that day. The toilet seat was broken, and propped up on the window sill which overlooked the yard. I glanced out of the window for Provena and Nita, the neighbours' children, to see if they were in their garden. It was cold sitting on the enamel toilet. When I used the last piece of toilet paper, a bright red streak of blood stained it. Looking down at my pants, I saw another trickle of blood on them. I quickly searched under Mom-mi's bed for more paper and scrunched this up before putting it inside my pants. I left the house then to go to the Wednesday club in the church opposite.

If I sat up straight, answered the questions correctly and sang in the choir, I could get some sweets, sherberts, cola bottles and chewits, also a stamp on my card which I could redeem for books. I always tried hard to be good when I went to the club, but more often than not I ended up being told to leave so you can guess what happened that particular day! When Mom-mi found out I had started my period, all she said was, "No badda breed up in disya yard!" Meaning that I had better not get myself pregnant. I wasn't given any explanation about what had happened, why I was bleeding. I spent the next year looking under her bed, and scouring the house for sanitary towels. My period caught me unaware every time it arrived.

Back then …

Here we are …

Part II

My Redemption Years

For God so loved the world that He gave His only Son, that whoever believes in Him should not perish but have eternal life.
   John 3 : 16

Chapter Sixteen

Finding My Way Through The Wilderness

When Kay was two and Laura four years of age, I used to drop them off at the Our Saviour Church Of God near to where we lived, so that they could attend Sunday school and play with the other children. This also gave me the opportunity to sleep, safe in the knowledge that they would be happy and well fed. There was one family in particular who looked after them, and my friendship with the parents developed into a relationship of mutual respect. Despite living fifteen miles apart, this family had a significant and positive impact on my girls. Apart from all the meals they provided when I was too ill to cook for them, they also took Kay and Laura on family trips, on one occasion for six weeks on holiday in Europe. I will always be thankful to them.

Whilst the girls were 14 and 16 years of age growing up, and illness had turned me into a recluse, they moved in with this family from the church for Christmas and New Year so that I could again stay in bed. Shutting out the world, I had even by then stopped going to my blood sample appointments at the hospital. My echocardiogram and nerve conduction studies had shown that I was suffering from degenerative muscles on my right shoulder. Although my left one was the good side, my right arm and legs often gave way. There was nothing I could do about this, they felt loose, and floppy. I was also suffering from pins and needles which were excruciatingly painful. I no longer had any interest in food, I often felt nauseous and I retched repeatedly. I used to shiver and have chills. This meant that I refused to eat and drink. I didn't want to wash or take my medication, clean the house and cook. I didn't see my children from the moment they broke up from school that Christmas to when they returned on the fourth of January. I had crashed both physically, and mentally. I stank of diarrhea, and stale blood. I scratched myself. I ignored the telephone when it rang and the curtains were left permanently closed. I felt again that I was ready to die.

Throughout this period and the following year, the girls didn't receive any gifts from me, not at Christmas, on their birthdays or at any other time. They walked two miles to school and back during the week, had irregular meals, wore dirty clothes or those in the lost and found box at school. I completely ignored their needs, and this is a debt which I now cannot repay. I still continue to thank them to this day. Despite all of the love I have for them, at the time, they were revising for their GCSE examinations and the house was bitterly cold. I remember that we used to huddle together in one room to try and keep warm. Despite being teenagers, they had overnight turned into my carers.

Even though the curtains were drawn all day, the debt collectors and bailiffs who congregated outside knew we were at home. We ignored them. We hid ourselves so that they couldn't see us. They wanted to serve a set of Court papers on me from one of the utility companies I owed money to. They gave up after a while and pushed the documents through the letterbox. I had made so many applications for back-dated maintenance in the past that I recognized the process servers when they rang the doorbell.

Several of the congregation from the Our Saviour Church Of God arrived at ten o'clock one evening with bags of shopping and a small amount of cash for us. They had done a charity walk to raise funds. I made a roast dinner from what they had brought, with all the trimmings. At half past two in the morning, we ate for the first time on my Katie Price glass and leather table. I watched my children eat the food ravenously as I told them how special they were and that I hadn't expected my life to be the way it was, let alone have cancer. They listened and seemed to understand. I didn't expect that nine months later they would be shouting at me about the adverse impact I had on their lives. I told them afterwards when we were having counselling sessions that God came first, followed by their nanny and them. Anything or anyone else didn't matter! They repeated the words effortlessly, and this became our mantra in every prayer we said after that.

In the end, my Mother came to live with us for five weeks, giving my children advice about the world at meal times; she also talked about my relationship with them. Being an old rebel herself wouldn't have made her the ideal person in the past to speak to us in this way, except that the earlier version of her had now been replaced by a vulnerable, gentle and caring woman who only had an occasional outburst. My children called her Nanny while she would always be Mom-mi to me. She explained to the girls that, even though I was their mother and had them to think about, I would still give all of my money to others, simply because I was a "giver" and others were "takers." My mother told my children that I needed to remember not everyone in life whom I helped to support would reciprocate when I needed it. Whether this was in respect of a financial, emotional or physical need. People had selective memories when it came to illness and money.

I fell asleep as she reiterated her values, and educated my children in the ways of the world. God did come first, then our family and, at that time, not money. My daughters were six feet tall at sixteen and eighteen years of age. They laughed while Mom-mi exaggerated my appalling behaviour at school, and at home when I was a child. She regaled them with tales of her parents' attitude to life, and her thoughts on Jamaica. She failed to mention the Big Daddy throws, or punches I had received from her, but never had those teenagers sitting around my Katie Price dining room table heard so many wise words from their grandmother. The same as I had listened to as a child years ago, between her punches and kicks.

My thoughts returned again to the past... A small parcel had arrived for her one day and she opened it carefully. "What's this?" I asked, impatiently.

"Sum tink your Aunty bring," Mom-mi said, kissing her teeth, before continuing to curse the cat.

Whatever it was smelt sickly sweet, and felt hard through the white napkins in which it had been loosely wrapped. I could tell that it was made from different pastel colours when I looked more closely. Unable to wait any longer, I pulled the first napkin away from it, and the entire package opened of its own accord. It looked like all of the icing you would find on a wedding cake had been pressed into a strangely shaped ball, without any of the cake. I was right. Someone had attached a bride and groom ornament to the icing. I looked at Mom-mi and our hearts sank. The other members of our family had gone to a party after the wedding, seen the flowers and the bride's dress. There would have been dancing too while our branch of the family had received a ball of discarded icing; nothing else, and certainly not an invitation.

My Aunts and Uncles lived within a ten mile radius of our house, we often bumped into them. Most of my cousins were older than my siblings and I. They had yellow skin, and afro hair which was soft and smooth in a loose curl pattern. Their lives had been very different from ours. They experienced years of dancing and singing lessons. Both families owned a car and they went to restaurants. They clearly believed that they were much better than us. As this was Mom-mi's family too, it was very wrong. I couldn't understand at the time why they did this, that whatever they were doing should justify Mom-mi being told only the briefest of details about it. Also that none of us were invited to attend any of their family events. It always happened like this. Even if they had spoken to us a few days beforehand, it seemed that every effort was made to ensure we did not mix with them, or become integrated into their lives.

This situation continued throughout the years I was growing up. The irony was that these cousins more often than not found their way back to Mom-mi to ask for emotional support if their own parents had become ill later on and unable to help them. Looking back now, it seems strange how life flipped a switch.

Those who had scorned and excluded us still relied on my mother to help them when they had in the past thought they were far too good to associate with our branch of the family. "Tan and see, watch the salvation!" Mom-mi used to say when we talked about them.

Chapter Seventeen

Reflections

I looked at the past, present and future with different eyes once I had faith in God and accepted His presence in my life. I believe now that Jesus really does exist, and cares about us. How do I know this? My life is a testimony to all He has done for me. Who else would have been strong enough to subdue my enemies, change the horrendous conditions in which I lived, give me healing and peace of mind? Being the black sheep of the family, the person whom everyone else avoided, even if only because of a grudge held years ago, eventually had a negative effect on me. Until I learned from prayer, research and thought, that being ostracised and ignored could also have its advantages. It freed me from the constraints of others. I had time to reflect, move forward and try new things when I was alone without having to seek approval from those who would no doubt have judged me, pulled me down or blasted me out the water for daring to be myself. Instead I was given the opportunity and time to think about the limitations they had previously set in their behaviour towards me; that it was important not to let the fear of being alone allow me to be swept into a physical or emotional relationship, with a single person or group, whom I suspected might be toxic.

Just as, in the same way, a small stream fights its way to the ocean, overflowing hills and gathering speed when it travels downhill, tossing and turning the debris along its path, it shuttles itself through valleys and mountains in a hurry to reach the greater expanse of sea, I believe that we often rush through life in a similar way. The good things which happen inside of us whilst we are swept along through the peaks and lows to the next big event might mean we never get to our ocean, but stagnate if we become too comfortable at the highest point in our lives, or later be anxious and fearful in our surroundings, as we are pushed further into old age and ultimately death.

Of course, we want to be happy and have it all, a partner, the nice house, children, business contacts and hits on social media. We want to stand beside those who already have what we desire, whatever it might take to achieve this, theft, lies, imagination, selling out and so on. We want! We want! We want! We want! Anyone not in the race will be tossed to one side.

Some lives become settled like lakes, with a monastery calm in serene surroundings. These have healthy horizons and powder blue sky outlooks, with only the faint sound of a burbling stream in the distance. The tired and weary pass by to rest on the lake's solid stones along the wavy edge of the water, slipping off their shoes for a short while before catching their breath and moving on, mesmerised by the silver light as it descends onto the shimmering water and flecks of orange seen beneath it like a mob of butterflies playing gleefully. Tiny ripples of life going about their day, its eldritch beauty soaked into the skin of its visitors; happy to remain where they are in life unless change rears its ugly head. When that happens even the lakes get swept into the ocean.

Just the same as when God intends to move us, needs our attention or wants to challenge us, He creates and changes our circumstances. In the same way as it happened to me, this is a test. He may remove all of our comforts, a house, job or car, replacing them with illness, financial and emotional problems, even the people in our life, including friends and family, so that we don't have a choice, only to focus on Him. That's why I am thankful to Him for giving me cancer. Before this I was blind, ungrateful, ignorant and selfish. I didn't have any idea of what I was doing to myself and others; sin had consumed my every thought, action and deed.

I had become disillusioned with the Church, the place where I expected to find solace, so much so that I believed suicide was my only friend. It would gently whisper to me, softly massaging my mind while it was numb with pain. Even the thought of going to Church filled me with dread. My body could enter the building but my heart was broken. The Church folk were pleasant enough but always left me feeling confused. The huge effort they made to get dressed up in the right shoes, clothes and hats, you would have thought that it was a day at Ascot, and the women had to have a firm grip on their husbands, especially those who had better jobs. Any attempt at having a conversation with one of them, taken any further than "Praise the Lord," would be met with a sour face or pursed lip. A baby might even be thrust into his hands to remind him that he belonged to her, and everyone else should back off. After all, men like them were scarce! Whilst the Bishops, Ministers' first ladies and Evangelists were the "crème de la creme" of Church society. Everyone wanted to be in their orbit; to give them something or talk to them. I felt sometimes that they were treated like Gods, and they definitely weren't that.

    These "nice nasties" knew that they could subject everyone else to their superiority, with fake dipped eye smiles, they had a lot of practice at ignoring others while they carried on gossiping. This seemed to me to be a type of bullying but it wasn't possible to complain. I couldn't take this issue to the Bishop or any of the Ministers to resolve. Their public presence alone reminded everyone that they had been praising the Lord, often for a good many years. Their children and siblings were also treated like royalty. Attending some of the churches was like going to a football match. Once you entered the stadium and took your seat, the crew or their families would always be given the top box so that they could look down on everyone else after they had shimmered past them in their Sunday best, those glorious wigs, best weaves, glistening nails and the highest of heels. Whilst the throng of the spectators cheered on the players, namely the Bishop, Ministers, Missionaries and First Ladies in charge of this or that, the huge roars of praise heaped on them seemed to me to be like chanting from the terraces. The players held the audience's attention, whooping and cheering intermittently. The Bible was not even opened, nor was a verse heard in the continual praise of their trips abroad, monies needed for a new roof or church, a special visitor who would be doing this and that.

So many other people who had relevant skills, sat in the audience, with their good ideas on how to move the church forward. They could easily have helped but the "nice nasties" had done their homework in pretending to make everyone feel welcome. They were pleasant to our faces but every conversation we had was fed back to the Church leaders who then picked, popped and placed us. Were we worthy to be in their group? Did we fit the part? Or in other words, did we bring status to their church?

Unfortunately, whilst this was going on, the truly sick, poor, and needy, were treated as mere hindrances by the coveted circle, unless the offerings intended for them were needed elsewhere. They also made good seat warmers, looked great on a Church seat, and helped to make the congregation seem full. Ironically, those who needed it most were not offered any real involvement in what was going to happen, and usually left because of bullying by their peers. Occasionally we might have been allowed to share a testimony or reading, get involved in the catering or cleaning, but we couldn't ask any questions. Definitely not pass on any of our ideas or challenge anything which had been said, even if this was done for the purposes of discussion or development.

If you are part of a Church congregation and your Bishop, Ministers and Church brethren pass beyond, "Praise The Lord" to actually talk to you, with Bible verse and prayer, then trust me you are a member of a good Church. When I was struggling through illness, someone might have asked me how they could support me? Would I have liked to discuss a particular topic or bible verse? Should we pray together? This was the number to call if I had any problems. He or she could support me, pray with me, even visit me. The only one who did this was Tiyanna, later on, in the Church I currently attend. She was a member of my Bible study class, not part of this higher echelon of Church society!

She also didn't agree with the new trend of seniors who always sat at the front in some Churches, arrived in the middle of a service to rip roaring praise, and entered the Church as if they were on a red carpet. The service couldn't start until after their arrival, with the name of each senior member being called out and praised before it began, even though the rest of us may have been waiting for an hour or more. It was also usual practice for them to carry on sitting in their elevated seats after the service ended. This gave the other Church members an opportunity to flock to them to touch, thrust money into their hands, or congratulate them on simply attending church. If I saw the same people in the supermarket the following day, they would pass me by, completely ignoring the fact that they knew me. Praise The Lord indeed! You might also see them at a conference later, or need a few details for an event they were organising yet, despite having all the information including the time it started, they maintained that they couldn't remember anything at all.

People going to football matches cheered for their team and meticulously followed each game, eager to know more about the opposition. They bought the merchandise, hats and T shirts because they wanted to be recognised as a supporter, often prepared to fight for the players against a rival team, especially if they didn't get the right result, or their opponent had the upper hand, and they felt cheated, always proud, eager to share and passionately discuss the team's performance. Along with the new players and past games, any great goals scored would be remembered and treasured, to pass down through the generations, the old, and young, united for the team. Men and women filled the terraces; it didn't matter that most were strangers to each other. They roared, sang, clasped hands, hugged and even cried together for their team, not afraid to say that they loved the players, talk about how the game was played and the future they wanted for the team.

Most of the Churches I attended lacked this level of enthusiasm, and I had been to a number of them. The insiders and new members, depending on how they had been recruited, would very rarely leave their comfort zone to win new converts to Christ. Standing in the streets on busy Friday and Saturday nights, or visiting a nightclub and public house to talk about religion, would be considered extreme. Whilst I have always believed that these are the real recruitment sites for new followers of Jesus.

I believe that everyone should be required to preach the word of the Lord, and share the Gospel, to bring people to the Lord. Words of encouragement need to be given to complete strangers, not the private details of a Church member's troubles, without any feelings of shame about doing this. There shouldn't be any schisms but a special anointing of the Holy Spirit in Jesus' name on Christ's messengers, the Bishop's preachers, teachers and so on who are delivering God's word with holiness. Also, with the ability to understand the scriptures and break them down, so that they can touch the heart of every listener.

It saddens me that most people, after being invited to a particular Church, give the same reasons why they won't regularly attend the services. "Dem black people dem chat your business and run you down... Dem Church people sit down quiet but dem devil underneath... They are only Christian in Church, but treat you bad when outside... Dem teef, only want you money... Dem judgmental, and show off... Dem Church people are de nastiest people me ever meet. Dem do me bad... Dem people just pimping the old and vulnerable for money... It's not warm, or inviting, but hit and miss how you are treated."

And yet, just like me, these are often the people who are broken and need the most help. The ones searching for their ocean through drugs or alcohol, brief sexual relationships and materialism, all of which they believe, or once believed, would make them happy, but have instead caused them to carry the same unresolved baggage into a new situation, relationship or environment. God showed me that, if things were not working out, then He would move us forward in life through change.

Chapter Eighteen

My Bible Study Class

The Bishop of the new Church I was attending persuaded me to go to the Bible study class. I didn't think I would like it, but I was on such a low ebb, that it became a case of why not? Easier than trying to explain again why I didn't think this would be for me. After all, as he pointed out, I read my Bible every day and wouldn't be without it, so why not share my faith with others? God also clearly had other plans for me when I met Tiyanna Reid, the woman who sat quietly in her usual seat at every single Bible class. I can't tell you now much of what Bishop ABC had to say; this was his nickname. I never found out why, but I loved listening to Tiyanna's gentle voice, when she shared with the five of us in the group, what she felt about God and His words in the Bible. What she said made a lot of sense to me once it was put in the context of everyday life. I used to go home after listening to her with so much more to think about.

When I had been attending the meetings for a few weeks, the Bishop started asking me to share my thoughts. He had previously let me get away with saying nothing but it was obvious now that I was going to have to contribute something of my own. However I might be feeling, he also explained to me that I had to be baptised again, as I was no longer attending a trinitarian church. I used to listen to his calm voice while he encouraged me to repent my sins by being baptised in the name of Jesus Christ, and receive the gift of the Holy Spirit.

I began by saying a little about the research I had been doing into the meaning behind the Bible quotations he gave us to discuss. It was then that I caught Tiyanna looking at me thoughtfully. Before that, all she had done was nod at me. When I sat down in what had become my usual chair, and she said hello along with the others, I did wonder at first whether she might be one of those people who thought they were better than everyone else, but this was far from the truth. I didn't find out until much later why Tiyanna was a self-contained person until she got to know someone, and could tell that you shared the same love of God's word as she did.

One day in late November, when she was putting her coat on to leave the hall where we met for the class, I said on the spur of the moment, "Do you fancy a cup of tea? Only if you have time, of course... I'd like to hear more about your thoughts on St. Peter." The last few words came out in a loud rush which made her smile, but that was it! The floodgates of our friendship had opened. Having a cup of tea with her after the Bible class became a regular occurrence. Tiyanna had also been through an abusive marriage, in which she wasn't allowed to voice an opinion, and for a long time afterwards had been afraid to speak, believing that she didn't have the right to say anything at all, having also learned early on the consequences of stepping out of line. As it turned out, we had a lot in common.

We soon became regular customers at the community cafe down the road, run by Frank, a Jamaican man, and for us to indulge more often than not in a slice of cake. I loved his homemade chocolate cake. Tiyanna preferred carrot cake, or a slice of Victoria sandwich from which strawberry jam oozed. This led on to us sometimes meeting for lunch before the class started. Tiyanna simply loved food, especially boiled dumplings, cho cho pumpkin, ackee, oxtail soft red rice, and the coconut drops she made, whilst I thought Frank's jerk chicken was incredible! You could taste the herbs he had marinated it in when he served it with a plate of rice and peas. He was a jovial man, and always had a big smile for us when we opened the door to the café no matter how busy he might be. He clearly loved what he did, and told me one day that he believed cooking for others was the Lord's work. Tiyanna thought that he tried to feed his customers' souls, not only their bodies, sharing his skills as a cook with those who needed them the most.

I started to get used to being around people again in his café, All sorts. While Tiyanna helped me so much to get back on track and no longer feel that there wasn't any point to life, it came as quite a shock to realise that I hadn't actually had a friend like this since Angelica at school. She had gone to live in the Caribbean after her marriage and we had drifted apart. I knew that this was mostly my fault for being too preoccupied with my own life but then it can be difficult to see things which aren't directly under our noses at the time. Tiyanna was a lot like her. Our friendship made me realise just how important the connections we make to others in life truly are; that the best of these can help us get through the dark times.

As we sat and talked, I told her about my family, and the way they had treated my parents. I could see it happening. I was turning into my Mom in the way the next generation behaved towards my children and I. The not to be forgotten slights, constantly changing their loyalty groups, and decisions regarding who to exclude; being perfectly pleasant with strangers, but regarding my branch of the family, it was a completely different matter. They would slit their own parent's throats if it made them top dog, even including those who might still be abroad, up north or down south, that didn't matter, if they had something against the other person. They sat like children waiting for a bedtime story on the latest fall out or fall in. Should we accidentally bump into one another, this process was now running three generations deep from the same behaviour I had witnessed my Aunts and Uncles directing at my Mother. Years later I had found myself in exactly the same position as she was but with my own siblings and extended family members hovering at the door in their Sunday best.

As a result of the stress all this caused, coupled with depression and anxiety, my weight had increased from nine and a half to thirteen stone in twelve months. It was only when I started reading the Bible that I understood. Attending the bible study group and talking to Tiyanna had opened my eyes. She allowed me to be myself when I was with her, and she made me realise that my unconfessed sins had become a barrier to my prayers. Discussing my feelings and personal circumstances, with someone who had unexpectedly entered my life, taught me so much. The bible study group became the allies I didn't know I would have, challenging my beliefs, choices, behaviour and decisions. God truly worked in a mysterious way through them.

I didn't know at first that Tiyanna had a sister. Looking back she didn't really talk a lot about herself, probably because I said enough for both of us, and she was such a good listener! It came as a surprise when she asked if we could meet again at the cafe. We had already had our weekly bible class and lunch there that week. She broke the bad news after we sat down and were drinking tea. "The thing is, Jane, I may not have mentioned it but I have a sister." Tiyanna sighed deeply. "Nancy has had a bad accident and won't have anyone to look after her when she comes out of hospital. We didn't really get on when we were growing up, but I am all she has now that our parents are dead. She didn't marry and doesn't have any children. I have been praying for her non-stop but it looks as if God wants me now to move to London to stay with her." Tiyanna smiled sadly. "I'm not going to be able to see as much of you for a while."

My heart felt as if someone had taken a sledge hammer to it as she was saying the words. "When are you going?" I asked in a voice unlike my own.

"On Friday," Tiyanna replied. "She'll be out of hospital during the afternoon. It's going to be a while before she's on the mend again, Jane. Oh, I don't know! I'll have to give up my flat here. I can't afford to keep it on. I need to help pay our living expenses but you'll still have the class," she continued quickly, after seeing my stricken face. "And we will both have our bibles."

I came back to reality then, and saw how the light in her eyes filled the crowded room, so strong was her faith. It reminded me that I wasn't going to be alone when she left for London. *God would still be with me.* How I wished in that particular moment I could simply accept this without Him having to carry on reminding me. "We can stay in touch on Whatsapp, and meet up as often as we can," Tiyanna said, trying to sound enthusiastic.

Nevertheless, as often happens in life, things didn't work out that way. Tiyanna decided to stay with her sister and not move back to Birmingham. My personal circumstances meant that I couldn't travel to meet her and we gradually contacted each other less and less, until one day many months later, I realised that I hadn't heard from her for a long time, neither had I sent her any messages.

Chapter Nineteen

I Lost My Faith In Him

God had sent Tiyanna to me when I most needed a friend. I wished I could have helped her in the same way as she helped me. She was such a good person, and after a while, I began to question my faith in Him again. I soon learned what was about to happen to me next, that it was back! I was on the verge of another bout of depression. I desperately asked God why, and to help me. I felt lost and very much alone. I believed that I couldn't cope with it happening again. My stomach began churning every day, my face had become drained of colour. I could no longer control my thoughts, they were drawn to it, the sense of loss and loneliness which was overwhelming me again. I lost my appetite. I wasn't interested in what anyone said. I couldn't be bothered to wash, eat or communicate in any way with anyone else. I had stopped going to the bible study class, and Frank's cafe. Tiyanna had gone too! How could I depend on God when I felt as if I had been abandoned?

My prayers became muddled. I knew that I had to believe and have faith to get through this again. However, it was easier said than done. He would make it better, He had my interests at heart. Everything was going to be okay, but I needed it to be now during this middle ground I still had to get through. I had suffered from depression for too long. Although I knew a lot of people I could talk to, I still couldn't explain this to them. It had reached the point that I felt I was only alive when facing adversity, in a dispute with someone else, listening to others complain, or planning a strategy to remedy a situation. Fully clothed and unable to cope, I threw myself onto the bed weeping. I curled into a ball and pushed the cushion into my chest for security and reassurance.

If I admitted this to anyone else, they would have thought I was crazy! The devils which pursued me had told me this often enough but I knew deep down I was not insane. I was only trying to cope with another episode of depression. I felt tired, really tired, emotional and anxious. I was a Christian, and had been baptised, so should I be experiencing this? I was desperately seeking deliverance from it whilst the Devil whispered to me to abandon my faith. God would not be coming this time to save me. I couldn't understand why Satan was using a loudspeaker in my ear and God's voice had become so distant.

I spent the entire day in bed without washing, getting dressed or feeding myself. All the cognitive behavioural sessions I had attended as part of my cancer journey, and the strategies I learned, fell by the wayside. I remembered being told to believe I wasn't alone; thousands of people at different stages in their lives suffered from depression, and far worse. I tried to focus on doing one thing which I enjoyed, to zone completely into this one activity. I tossed my head back and reached for my bible, that I had intended to read that day, even if I could now only manage a single verse of it. Simply holding and attempting to open the bible, then flick through the pages, was a huge effort.

Until God answered me, when I came across Samuel 1. I sat upright on the bed. It was as if someone had switched on the light. I was soon engrossed in this bible story. Who were King Saul; Jonathon, and King David? I could not put it down; it was as if my mind had turned a somersault. I had been going to church all my life, participating in events and I listened carefully to the services every week. I had even endured my holier than thou Church sisters but it was reading while at my lowest ebb that I truly began my recovery. It gave me a longing to be in our Almighty Father's presence. My bible reading became insatiable. I was transfixed, and could not put it down. When I did, it was only to research opinions on the verses and their meaning or to review calendars and maps, to gain a much better insight into the era when the stories were set.

I slowly began to feel better. I started by repeating the mantra that this was just a single episode in my depression. I repeated it continually, only stopping when my Obsessive Compulsive Disorder kicked in. I cleaned every room in the house again, using undiluted bleach, so that I could go back to reading the bible as quickly as possible. I read about how others had coped with difficult situations, like King David ministering to himself, although I didn't fully understand this at the time. How Elijah became discouraged, weary and afraid after great spiritual victories over the prophets of Baal; this mighty man of God had run for his life, far away from the threats of Jezebel. He sat down and prayed in the desert when he was defeated and exhausted.

I thought too of Job and all the trials and tribulations he suffered. Jeremiah wrestled with great loneliness, feelings of defeat and insecurity. Also known as the weeping Prophet, he suffered from constant rejection by the people he loved and reached out to. God had called him to preach, yet forbidden him to marry and have children, so he lived alone. He ministered alone, he was poor, ridiculed and rejected by his people. In the midst of all this, he displayed great spiritual faith and strength but I could also see his honesty in the bible when he wrestled with despair and a sense of failure.

As the day wore on, I eventually accepted I had to believe God's mercy reigned, even during times like this when I was feeling broken. *Reading the bible opened my eyes to the fact that I didn't know as much as I thought I did.* I would need to start again from the beginning so I began to research with a notepad, pen and my laptop. What exactly was mercy and grace, all the different names people used for God, and Jesus? What were the meanings behind these? When I went to Church the next day, I listened to the young people and let them become my teachers. Whilst I was their pupil, taking notes in my search to establish a good relationship with God, I desperately wanted to transform myself, and lead a Christian life from that moment on.

In all of the bible stories I read that day, God was always nearby. He was there on the good days and during the dark times too. He didn't condemn those in the bible for their questions or pain. He didn't tell them to get on with it; he reached down instead into their deepest suffering and lifted them from it. He cared, He showed compassion, He offered mercy. He brought hope and instilled purpose. He gave victory, and He still works in the same way today. Our world desperately needs those who give joy to others and bring hope to the people who believe there is none left; those in our lives who help us remember the meaning of real grace, and where lasting help might be found, just as Tiyanna had helped me.

The greatest truth is this. We have a Saviour who understands our pain. He is aware of every weakness and hurt we suffer. He reaches out to us with compassion and hope. He is a healer, redeemer and restorer, our friend. He would never waste the seasons of suffering we faced, but use them instead to bring good into the world; also to instil purpose to help others and make us stronger. Depression is a common illness affecting many people, and is treatable. Yet statistics had shown me that only one third of those who were suffering from it received any treatment.

Whilst all of us carry baggage through our lives from unresolved issues, disappointment and hurt, bruises from the past and living only for today, we expect to magically meet Mr Right then live happily ever after.
No, Sir!
If the starting point within ourselves and foundation isn't fully healed, how can we expect to meet that special someone and for it to be perfect? A great relationship will not come from false foundations. This applies to any relationship, not only romantically, also with the people at work, in a local shop or restaurant, our character and hurt follow us wherever we go.

Chapter Twenty

Life In Jamaica Before I Was Born

I realised eventually that what happened before I was born had also helped make me the person I was. What my parents had experienced and learned, they in turn passed on to their children. It was my choice then, as an adult, whether I continued in the same way as had always been done in our family, or I changed. The possibilities for change were endless, especially with God's help.

When I was a young, I loved my brown moccasin clunky shoes with their tractor tyre heels. I wore a light blue blouse and a chequered green skirt. My elder sister's hand-me downs were far too short in the arms and legs but the body part fitted me. I was so proud of her rara skirt, I can still see it now. My clothes were a complete mish-mash, often out of season, but I didn't care. As long as I could play outside, there wasn't any reason to stay in, only Dad-di lying on the foam settee, listening to the cricket on the television and radio. Despite this, he made the best beans and eggs. My sisters and I would fight afterwards over who would get the frying pan, while the onions in his ackee and saltfish were so sweet. He was a much better cook than Mommi. The only time we would get proper boiled dumplings was if he made them before his night shift.

Dad-di was at his happiest, when tending his two meter garden patch behind our house. It was his little bit of Jamaica, the acres upon acres he still owned in Trelawney and Jacksonville. He paid the taxes every year to keep them going. During all the years he lived in the United Kingdom, I know how much he used to worry about the lush green vegetation, rich in mangoes, avocados, oranges, and lots more. Those beautiful, sprawling acres he had left behind, the tiny shack made of corrugated iron, with its dust floor he still called home. The time he had spent as a boy working in the fields, looking after the sheep, cows and goats. After a while, his mouth became permanently turned down, like a sad fish who could only dream of the warm seas where it used to swim.

He very rarely used his false teeth but if he was with my daughters, his grandchildren, he used to pull them out of his pocket when they least expected him to, especially on formal occasions, and this was usually accompanied by hysterical laughter. He was doing it in every Christmas photograph we took, with his feet crossed and one thumb up. He was a real grandparent to my children, something which I did not experience. He took huge delight in going to the children's plays and performances, picking them up from the private nursery I had sent them to, also gave him enormous pleasure. In fact, nothing was too difficult for my parents to do when it came to my children. They gave us tremendous physical and emotional support while the girls were growing up, making sure that I didn't have to buy school uniforms well in advance, so that their school clothes would be far too big for them to wear. They bought everything as it was needed, and Mom always looked for a bargain. They used to take the girls for a walk in the park or go shopping with them, do the cooking, cleaning and help with whatever was required. Once I got in from work, I took over from them. I also made sure that all of us had a full two weeks holiday at Easter in a different place every year, ranging from Gran Canaria, Egypt, Greece to Italy. I showed my gratitude to them in this way and I am so glad now that I did.

Watching my Father navigate a pram with a nine month old baby inside was hilarious. He would practice putting it up and down, removing and opening the plastic cover in case it rained, as Laura and Kay crawled in and out of it. Their grandmother would over feed them lovingly with bottles of milk, often Milo chocolate milk. They used to be dressed in exactly the same outfits, usually from Monsoon, Harvey Nichols or other boutiques if it was a special occasion, with Mothercare, Marks & Spencer, Gap and Next clothes for everyday. Being bi-racial, I separated their hair into tiny plaits and they chose their own bobbles. I knew that once I dropped them off at five-thirty in the morning, they would be okay, my parents would collect them later from the nursery. For a long time I had doubts about the long periods of time they had spent in childcare, whether it was all worthwhile, until I realised that only God could answer this question. None of us can change the past. Being a single parent was really tough; all those decisions which had to be made alone with no one to share or bounce ideas off. My adult life became a treadmill of work and parenting. I pray now that when they are older, they won't be alone and God will give them a good Boaz. Also that they will have compassion for me as a mother, who did her best in juggling all the balls she had been given.

Our family roots are most definitely in Jamaica. My mother who is now in her eighties still talks about her life there while she was growing up, and it's good to know more about it. What she told me has in many ways helped me put my own life into perspective. I like to think about this beautiful island in the Caribbean where my family came from. Also to remember everything my Father and her went through, to make a better life for all us in England. I will always be grateful to them for this.

They didn't have luxuries when they were young, and grew their own food on the dirt track which led to the school in Thatchfield. Corn, pears, mangoes, apples, lemons and oranges, tangerines, bananas, avocados, cocoa beans and coffee, sugar cane, sweet potatoes and yams. My Mother's parents, Una and Arnold Williams, were self-sufficient. Along with their neighbours, they had a flour mill on their land, but didn't have any machinery to work it. Everything had to be done by hand with a hoe, sickle and garden fork. The parish of Thatchfield where they lived is in Saint Ann on the north east coast of Jamaica. It is the largest one on the island and is often called the Garden parish for its natural beauty, also because anything planted there seems to grow easily, especially the flowers. High up in the mountains the greenery is dense and hot underneath the intense sun. Mom-mi told me that the oranges and lemons she grew when she lived in Thatchfield were the size of Dad-di's fist! Grandfather Arnold was a farmer. He kept a variety of animals, pigs and cows, goats, chickens, donkeys and mules. There was a slaughter-house on his patch of land, but he didn't have access to a water tank which could be used for the animals' drinking water. This had to be carried in large drums before and after school.

My mother was born on the seventeenth July nineteen forty. She had one good outfit for going to Church and a school uniform in blue and yellow; this had been handmade from flour bags. Apart from that, the only clothing she owned was a single house dress which was washed in the evening so that it would be dry by morning, and ready to wear again. A broken tree branch with a piece of string attached served as a coat hanger. The family shared a ten acre plot of land with their neighbours, all of whom had built a couple of outbuildings, and lived in one of them. This was similar to a wooden shed with a zinc corrugated roof and a single room inside. There was usually a table, one large bed and two seats for any officials or the ministers if they called. The fire in the grate always had coffee brewing. Most of the time the occupants of these homes ate with their fingers while sitting on the floor; cups, saucers and plates were kept for visitors.

Mom-mi said that they always knew what to expect for each meal, depending on which day of the week it was. On Monday there would be mutton soup, Tuesday it was cabbage and fish, whilst Wednesday was tripe and Thursday pork, followed by liver and light rice on Friday, and Saturday cow foot soup. The weekly visit to the market in Brownstown, to sell and trade the animals, involved a three hour walk there and back. Instead of buying a bottle of rum to take home later, my grandfather would often meet his friends who would get him drunk and take his money! He used to be violent when he came home, and break what they had inside the one room all of them lived in. Even though they didn't have a lot, he still managed to damage the table, shelves and cups.

My mother and her siblings were afraid of him, especially when he argued with Grandma Una. He didn't hurt Mom-mi because she had learned early on to do exactly as she was told, but the others hadn't. They got up to all sorts of mischief and were often beaten for it, tied firmly to one of the chairs and struck repeatedly with a cord or stripped back elastic branch, until their skin was red raw. It didn't matter how much this hurt, Mom-mi said that they still had to get up the next day at five o'clock in the morning to do the chores. The animals were waiting to be fed, water carried, potatoes dug, the cows milked, and so on. The list of chores was endless and a lot of the work was done in the dark. Nevertheless Grandma Una still expected the floor to be shiny when she inspected it, and she never did any of the work.

Mom-mi and her siblings were treated like slaves by Grandpa Arnold and her, not even having the freedom to walk to school. They had to run so that they would have enough time to do the chores which had been allocated to them. If they didn't finish them, they would be punished. Needless to say, they had very little love in their lives while they were growing up. Their parents didn't hug, kiss or have proper conversations with them. The focus was always on not answering back. The only games any of the children played were at school, volleyball, touch and run or marbles. If a baby was born, any of the holes in this single room had to be sealed. The mother and her baby would stay inside until he or she was at least four months old, without any inoculations, help from a midwife, or the child's name being put on a register of births like in the United Kingdom. After this the baby used to be strapped onto the woman's back, with the expectation that she would carry on working in the cornfield as usual.

One day Mom-mi was late for school and hid in the bushes, trying to avoid being punished. When she was caught the teacher stood on a bench and beat her repeatedly until her skin bled, using a piece of wood with nails in it. She still has the scar marks on her back. Later she was beaten again by Grandmother Una, but not Grandpa. No one was allowed to speak to her because of what she had done.

Grandma Una was born on the fifteenth May nineteen fifteen. She had two sisters called Lettie and Eliezer. The youngest was very rich later in life, and used to ask why Una had so many ugly children. She only liked the light skinned ones like herself. My

Grandma used to call them her inheritance. She didn't have a large house the same as her sister, with its own water tank, and the local children to do the cleaning if their parents owed money to her. Mostly though she was jealous of my Grandma Una because she couldn't have any children of her own. Una married Grandad Arnold when she was eighteen years old after being raised by an Uncle. Mom-mi told me she used to talk about how much her brothers loved her when she was a child.

Grandad Arnold was tall and slim. He was thought to be a good looking man, with European features and a straight nose, he could pass himself off as being white. He was born on twenty-first May nineteen hundred and one. His mother, Aunt Gemima, was Asian and dark skinned. She had long straight hair and was upset when he married Grandma Una whose skin was brown, not light as she had wanted it to be. Later, she would only acknowledge her lighter skinned grandchildren. She simply loathed dark skinned people.

Granddad Arnold came from a large family of nineteen siblings, mostly twins and triplets. He had a twin sister, Miriam. Grandma Una and Grandad Arnold had eleven children of their own, including my Mom. Grandma Una's sister, Aunty Roslyn, was a kind woman. She often helped wash her nieces' clothes and spent time teaching Mom-mi how to use a hoe; also to clean the wheel stool, removing any insects so that they couldn't eat the yams while they were still growing, pick the coffee beans, beating them until they were dry, separating the part which couldn't be used, grinding the beans then in the mortar, before parching them after they had warmed in the douchie pot, to make fresh coffee which was always on the hearth.

The discovery of bauxite on my family's land in the nineteen fifties made it valuable, and prompted my grandparents to work my Mother even harder than she already did. Bauxite rock soon became the primary source of income for local families and communities. Finding it created a lot of change. Huge, dirty, trucks and machinery began to make their way through the village. The noise they made could be heard in the distance.

Mom-mi can still remember the impact those large companies had on people's lives. When they began to mine the land in Thatchfield, the pickneys, or children, didn't want to go to school any more, once they realised they could earn money immediately, if they became part of the mining industry.

Mom-mi said that the water supply to the well they used, and the ones in other areas, would sometimes be cut off. People complained then about the miners taking the island's underwater resources from them. Thatchfield appeared in the Jamaica Gleaner, a local newspaper, after it had been seriously affected. The benefit to the local population of having a long line of trucks moving across their land could never out do Mom-mi's knowledge of the place where she was born. The green and dense forest or fields which the strangers mining bauxite called jungle, this was Mom-mi's Thatchfield Gully, and she was proud to call Jamaica her home.

Grandpa Arnold told his children that they had to go to school. It was important they learned to read and write, not abandon the opportunity of getting a good education, to do one of the jobs which the mining company had brought to the local community, driving a truck, or working in one of the new shops. Grandpa said that their school work had to come first whilst the sheer number of tasks which needed doing to keep the farm running carried on. They couldn't stop for regular meals or to go to Saint Ann's Bay and nearby Brownstown if they wanted to. People often used the sea to wash their clothes, and themselves, or as a source of food when they went fishing. Until bauxite was discovered, there was nothing else they could do except work on the land and look after the animals, every day after school.

Mom-mi knew the Saint Ann and Discovery Bay areas like the back of her hand. She used to wear a pinafore dress, without shoes or sunscreen, as she walked in the heat of the sun every day. Balancing sacks of fruit or water on top of her head, she would cut through the forest and make her way to Lime Tree Garden School. It was quicker to do this than follow the torturous tracks the tourist buses and work trucks used. The coastal resorts full of holiday makers eventually became her "curiosities."

She loved to look at the visitors. She can still remember the first time she wandered away from the market and saw a showroom dummy. It was made from white, shiny, plastic and seemed to be smooth, not like skin. A lady was dressing the dummy in clothes, as if it was a real person, before putting it in the shop window for all to see. Mom-mi soon learned that this was what the farmers were starting to call modern. The visitors to the Saint Ann area laughed a lot as they walked around half-naked, drinking alcohol and eating anything people brought onto the beach for them. They seemed to enjoy revealing nearly every centimeter of their skin. Mom-mi used to watch them, if she had time, which didn't often happen after school! The coffee was always waiting to be picked, along with the corn, whilst the oranges and lemons had to be gathered from the fields. The pigs and other animals also needed water. The list of chores remained endless.

Chapter Twenty-One

A New Life In England

Dad-di was born on the tenth May nineteen twenty-eight and called Ethelbert Campbell; he was also known as Cyl. He had an awful life after his parents died, growing up with Uncle Bertie and his wife, Aunt Adeline, who loathed him. His uncle was a trader in the United States of America, so not always at home. When my Grandmother Mary Ann was pregnant, she found out that her husband had an affair, so she left him and went to live with her brother Bertie, and Adeline. Dad-di wasn't allowed to go to school. He was expected instead to run the plantation farm and do the deliveries because of his uncle travelling abroad to work. Dad-di was sometimes beaten so badly that he lost consciousness. On one occasion Ms Adeline called the district council who threw a bucket of water over him, so that he would open his eyes again.

He was understandably a quiet child and barely spoke, working in the field for his uncle, on his own. He was unable to read or write and would visit Grandma Una to do odd jobs for her. That's where he met Mom when she was seven years old. Seeing how kind he was Mom-mi said that she was going to marry him, whilst my Dad, who was older than her, didn't take any notice. However, the entire district back then soon found out that this light skinned girl with a yellow face, brown freckles and ginger hair was going to marry Cyl. He was teased mercilessly about it.

Mom-mi told me how handsome she thought Dad-di was. She described what he looked like in the corn field one day. His skin had been blackened by the hot sun and she said he was covered in sweat, making his muscles more defined, with a light coloured moustache, his hair was in tight curls. Part of his job as a cultivator was to deliver food supplies to the schools in the district. Whenever he visited her school or Grandma Una, Mommi would catch his eye. He eventually made a promise to her that they would go to England, and come back to the land they both loved when he was eighty years old. Unfortunately, he died before this could happen.

No one married outside of the village back then, and Mommi and Dad-di didn't have a lot of time to spend with each other. Children were regarded as their parents' pension pot, someone to look after them in their old age. Grandma Una and Mom-mi's sisters believed that she would be the one to stay behind in Jamaica to look after them. Even when Mom and Dad were almost adults, they couldn't relax or have fun. Life was only for working on the farm every single day, morning, noon and night; it was always hard physical work. My great grandparents had been slaves, and it seemed as if Grandma Una and Grandpa Arnold had inherited the practice of cracking a whip, using whatever was nearby.

My father eventually ran off to England and began writing to my Mom. When she was sixteen years old, she overheard her sisters and Grandma Una saying "Look at her! She can't even wash her baggy pants. Who is she, to be getting a letter from England?" Ms Adeline tried to help them and she organised a job for Mom-mi, doing cleaning for the school teacher, a mean spirited woman who only allowed her to use one pot for powdered milk and cooking, but Mom was happy to go. There were huge opportunities by this time from Windrush. Ms Adeline also told Grandma Una not to hide her letters from Dad, but she didn't stop doing this. In the end Ms Adeline took Mom-mi to the local post office and told them to keep the letters safe until she could collect them herself.

When Dad-di was nineteen years old, he sent Mom a ticket so that she could travel to England and join him there. Again, with Ms Adeline's help, she managed to get a passport. My grandparents travelled with Mom on the back of a truck to Jamaica's Kingston airport. As the sixth child of nine, she had become a hard worker and they didn't want her to leave. She could clean the corrugated shack they lived in, peel yams and breadfruit, kill the chickens, then pluck and season them. All of which she did so quickly that they were soon in pots the size of sinks. She had also become known for her speed when milking the goats. You could always get a meal when she was there, whether or not it was cooking, and this strength was to serve her well in later life.

When she went to England, she eventually had five children to feed, before the age of twenty three. I can tell you now that she could throw cornflour into water and milk before school, to make the best cornmeal porridge we had tasted. There might sometimes be ackee and saltfish, but this was a luxury, with fried fritters that were half raw, and given to us like a burned offering. As you already know, her fried dumplings were as rock hard as bullets. The kitchen was always covered in flour, vegetable peel and water when she had finished. But all this was home cooked, and we didn't know any better. The only complaint we had was that there was never enough to go around! Grandpa Arnold's parting words to Mom-mi when she left Jamaica was that things would be different in England; she should only eat rice, vegetables and flour.

Later on, Grandma Una had to watch six of her children disappear from her life when they also left for England. The farm became desolate and the many acres unattended. They could no longer pile the children onto the back of a truck, or sometimes even walk the seventy miles with them to Kingston market at Saint Ann's Bay, carefully carrying the chickens' eggs.

When Dad arrived in England, he was unwell, uneducated and illiterate. Nevertheless, he found work in a foundry. One day he was left inside the hot furnace when it was switched on and he injured his back. My parents didn't have a lot of money but they had the most important thing... Each other! Mom-mi told me that they ate a lot of fish and chips at first since this was the staple diet of their new country. The accommodation which was available to rent had a double bed in every room. Those who worked the day shift slept in it at night, and were replaced by the night workers when they came in from work. The room my parents rented belonged to an era when landlords would often categorically state they wouldn't accept tenants who were Black, Irish or had dogs.

Mom-mi shared a single bed with Dad in a room which also had two double beds in it, used by complete strangers, but she was happy. It was the first time she had the opportunity to spend any real time with my Dad, and for there to be love in her life. She also liked experiencing the sights and smells of England which were quite different from Jamaica. Walking around the shops, she began to understand the tourists she had enjoyed watching at Discovery Bay and Ochi Rios. They were fully dressed this time, and had worn bikinis and little else whilst on holiday. My parents enjoyed browsing before going back to their room to fill the paraffin heater, and make toast on top of it.

After a while, they managed to buy a two up two down house, and sent for Mom-mi's sisters, Rosy and Dymond. Despite the number of times Mom-mi helped them get a job and places to live, they still became scornful when they were able to lead their own lives. They didn't tell her when they got married, or had children later on. They landed on their feet and gloated over my mother, only acknowledging the lighter children on our side of the family, and teasing my Mom for having too many children before her twenty-fifth birthday. A huge barrel of clothes was sent from Jamaica to my Mum on one occasion. Rosy and Dymond took the better items and gave the rest away. Mom-mi didn't find out about this until she was in Canada years later. Rosy was the worst. She had been the first one to arrive in England, and tried straightaway to take over Mom's life, pushing her way into the friendships she had made, her relationships with work colleagues, and she told everyone my mother's private business.

The betrayals were endless, stealing money, gloating about the restaurant she later ran, her children being at private school, and so on. Yet when she contracted Alzheimer's disease, her children, my cousins, asked my mother for help and advice, failing to remember how they had treated us in the past. The most hurtful part was when Dad-di was diagnosed as having senile dementia. We couldn't call any of them for help or support; neither did any of these close relatives visit him in the care home where he lived for seven months. Again they had forgotten how much we helped them when their parents needed care, despite some of them living hundreds of miles away from us. "Back on the shelf" was our common theme. Ignored, excluded and forgotten - then used and put back on the shelf to rot, unless needed again. I now understand the long pauses in conversations, lack of eye contact or infrequent face to face. Covid lockdowns were not around then but the restrictions then were similar to now, no communication or contact.

As you already know, Grandma Una came to England when she was elderly, and was given my single bed. She died some time later when my aunts and uncles were arguing with Mom-mi about where she should live. None of them had heard from her until she arrived that day, clearly unwell. She left seven acres in her will to each of her children. The land is in Knapdale, less than two miles from Brownstown, and the bequest remains in dispute. Some of my Mom's siblings have died, and my cousins claim that they have a right to the land as descendants of the deceased, while also, at the same time, denying our right to any of it. The irony is that Mom-mi is the one who continues to pay the land tax in Jamaica, and has done this for the last eleven years.

Part III

The True Meaning Of Love

Jesus said, " I am the way, and the truth, and the life. No one comes to the Father except through me."
John 14 : 6

Chapter Twenty-Two

The Generational Curse In My Family

My mother's sisters were the opposite of Dad-di and her. I suppose you could call them modern because they embraced contemporary culture before my parents did. It was easy to see the disdain on our cousins' faces when they looked at us sitting on the floor. We used to laugh when Mom-mi was trying her best to get them to sit down on the orange settee. If they couldn't avoid it, they would reluctantly sit on one of the arms, obviously under the impression that it was made of hard wood or had metal inside, and they would usually fall off when the soft foam didn't hold their weight.

On the rare occasions when we visited them, we used to think that they were posh. They had meals on plates, sitting properly around the table. We always sat on the floor with a plate on our laps, and only at the table if it was a special occasion. They even had salad and chips which we regarded as western food. The fizzy pop man came to their house too. Everything matched in their kitchen from the tiles to the table and chairs. I loved visiting them, even though they loathed me, because I was considered to be a troublemaker. They lived in new houses, and every item of clothing they wore also matched. We loved their toys, especially the dolls and bicycles. My aunts and uncles used to check that only my sisters were going to ride them, but they didn't know me! I would take the children a long way into the park so that I could grab one of the bicycles and ride it quickly. I didn't care if I was told off afterwards; I had too much fun doing it.

Their houses had neat gardens and trees. Everything, in every room, had its own place. There was enough space to walk between the furniture, and there definitely wasn't any clutter. The ornaments, trinkets and doilies were dust free. They had presents at Christmas and for birthdays, with parties, and brightly coloured wrapping paper especially made for children. It seemed incredible to us back then how much they had. None of it was shared with us, nor were we included in any of their fun. My aunt used to talk about her restaurant, all of the jobs waiting to be done, and complaining about how much she had to do. When I went there on one occasion, she didn't even offer me a glass of water. I saw boxes upon boxes of Walkers' crisps. The sweets she had on sale were my elder sister's favourite, and yet she didn't give us anything. We stood and watched her being friendly with the customers; she soon changed the tone in her voice when she wanted us to leave. We didn't get any of the acknowledgement or kindness she reserved for those strangers.

I had to watch my parents and siblings being treated badly by our relatives. I heard the pain in Mom-mi's voice when they left our house. I saw Dad-di roll his eyes, and still they breezed in and out with their tales. When they mentioned seeing old family friends from Jamaica, Mom-mi asked them to let her have a telephone number or an address so that she could also catch up on their news, but they ignored her, going instead into another one of their long drawn out stories. The way they completely ignored my father was even worse, not speaking or including him; it was as if he didn't exist. They only spoke to Mom-mi whom they seemed to think was the captain of our ship.

I remember the men talking about their jobs on the buses, the vacancies in the companies where they worked, or the public houses they frequented. They never once slapped Dad-di's back or invited him when they went for a drink. We knew exactly what they were doing, and they realised that we did, yet they still carried on. Mom-mi wouldn't let us say anything about it. They talked about a new car or fixtures and fittings in their houses while our parents were struggling to put food on the table to feed us. Irrespective of this, we were never once invited to stay overnight in any of their houses, nor did they even ask us how we were. This was definitely not the Cosby Show in which the uncles and aunts showed an interest in their nieces and nephews. Even though most of our cousins were the same age as us, with only two to five year gaps between, they didn't pass their hand-me-down clothes to our branch of the family or send food parcels, when it must have been quite clear to them how badly we were struggling.

I made a decision when I was a child that I would never again let people treat me like this, gloating about how much they had, and to make the situation even worse, their children were exactly the same. When we brushed past them, they would move closer to their parents, pulling in the side of their skirts or coats, as if we shouldn't even touch them. My older sister Grace used to ask when they left, what was the point of their visit if they only came to gloat. This was before she escaped, hopping and skipping out to America at the age of fourteen, after being sponsored by the Church.

We did sometimes go to our relatives' houses without being invited, and I liked to watch them making a drink in a glass cup. It fascinated me that, not only did all of the cups and saucers match, but there was cake too. They even had a biscuit tin; our eyes were transfixed when that came out! Whereas in reality, we were not going to be offered anything other than the two or three biscuits which they put in a napkin on a side plate next to us. We ate and swallowed these in seconds. We always waited for more, or at least being offered them, but this didn't happen. Instead we were told the time, and that our parents would be waiting for us. We didn't understand that this meant they wanted us to leave. Usually no longer than fifteen minutes later, we were taken to the door. No one patted us gently on the head, asked how we were, had a cosy chat with us, or picked us up and hugged us. There wasn't any kindness or love in our relationship with them, even though we were members of their family, and children who clearly needed their help.

I remember too that their houses were always clean and had coal fires. My cousins had their own bedrooms. We used to sit on one of the beds in a line in order of age while they stared at us. If we went near any of their toys, these were soon picked up and held. They also had matching quilts with themed covers, an abundance of crisps, sweets, and fresh towels and potions in their bathrooms. I would spend a long time washing my hands, putting the soft towel against my face, before being told abruptly that it was time to go. When I left these family homes I felt embarrassed, ashamed and very sad. As we walked away, we could hear their white friends and neighbours' children calling to ask them if they wanted to play outside. I watched my sisters looking back at them in the park, whizzing about on their bicycles, shouting and playing with their friends. They didn't understand that we were not considered good enough to play with our cousins although they realised that we were treated differently from the other children. They were unusually quiet when we walked home. I couldn't crack any of my usual jokes, tell a story or do the funny dance which made them laugh. I would have given anything I had back then to remove the despair and pain on their faces.

We had several sisters-in-law who were white. One in particular used to sit meekly on the settee with her head down. She had long blonde hair and a good relationship with Mom-mi. She ate whatever was put in front of her, always let the children play at her house as Mom-mi and her cooed over them. This sister-in-law gave us our very first wrapped Christmas presents, inside red, shiny metallic paper with a candle print; she gave everyone in the family a present. There was even a new coat, size twenty-six, for my Mother. Mom-mi held it up, and said, "Lord have mercy!" I will never forget how all of us opened those presents in slow motion. No one wanted to tear the paper, it was beautiful, and very precious. We were so happy simply holding it, and at last having something of our own.

This twenty-one year old woman had chosen a bright pink hat, matching scarf and gloves for me. Even though I was twelve years old, I had never received anything which matched; my gift was also new and clean, not forgetting bright pink! As each one of us carefully opened his or her present we "ooed" and "ahhed," before putting them back into the wrapping paper. Our sister-in-law stared at us when we did this, she didn't understand how we felt. She dressed her own children smartly in lightly coloured and bright clothes that again always matched each other. In all the time I knew her she barely spoke in the presence of my family. I had however overheard her outside, screaming at my brother when they visited us, the venomous tone in both their voices and the swear words they used, before they came into our house pushing the most beautiful pram.

As you know, when I had my daughters, I believed that I wasn't doing enough for them. There were many evenings driving home when I used to be crying inside. I knew that my children needed more of my physical attention while they were growing up, and I had to work to earn money for us to live on. I realised later that I had forgotten to teach them how to apologise and solve the problems they had, or to have compassion for their own. Nevertheless, I also watched the way my aunts and uncles behaved towards their children, the cousins who would scorn us, and later on, be estranged from their own parents only because of a misunderstanding, slight, or minor problem which could easily have been resolved with forgiveness and compassion. Instead my aunts and uncles had to wait while their children went through every family member they could, and reconnected with anyone whom they no longer had a relationship with; adults who had their own issues listened to their grievances, then fed the flames, creating another fracture of generational fall out. After a while, this damage ran so deep that years often passed, with a son or daughter spending the best part of his or her life with strangers. Those who would gloat, scorn and put their feet on the mother's neck, too hurt, tired or ashamed to reconnect with each other.

A lot of biracial children eventually drifted in and out of our branch of the family. As children we played outside with them. All of our first generation black male cousins, whom we would only see on rare occasions, had biracial children; there were nearly thirty of them, predominantly girls. They integrated with our side of the family, sitting with us in our chaos at home, and were always given preferential treatment to anyone who lived in the house. My Mom would cook, clean and act as a role model to these sixteen and seventeen year old girls. Their backgrounds often included care homes, prostitution or theft. For fifteen years or more we might be their only source of family, not having any contact with the caucasian side of their family, their aunts, uncles or grandparents.

They usually disappeared from our lives after this, rarely visiting us, and it was years before we discovered the reason. They had reconnected with their Caucasian family members. This meant they no longer wanted any communication with the black side of the family. It didn't seem to matter to them if this particular parent or relative was in prison, taking drugs, abused them verbally or let them down. It was perfectly clear to us that this was who they had chosen; their children were also not allowed to mix with us. On the rare occasions we did see them, they would not acknowledge us as their aunts. They used our first names instead, as a means of distancing themselves. It was, at the time, considered highly disrespectful to call any uncle or aunt by their first name if you were a first generation British child. Only when they had their own children and began to use the title of aunt amongst themselves, must they have understood the true meaning of their behaviour.

When we played outside with them in the street as a large group, they used to tell us how much they hated being black, especially their hair, and how their children were going to have straight hair. We could not understand this back then, and dismissed their comments as bizarre. It was strange to hear a five year old child saying things like that, especially when they were eating curried goat and rice as fast as they could, and drinking Guinness and carrot punch! My mother still sent presents to this endless stream of nieces and nephews, even after they no longer acknowledged us. As aunts we sent gifts at Christmas or on other special occasions, mostly without receiving the courtesy of a reply. Their caucasian partners were not allowed to meet or talk to us; in some cases, they didn't even know we existed. It was as if they had rewritten their past and any involvement we had in it. Were they truly afraid that this might reveal something which would compromise their relationship with the Caucasian part of the family?

Another generational level of dysfunction was urging them to do this. I know now that I should have reacted differently when it was happening. I should simply have said that I blessed them, and left them to their own lives. My faith in God has taught me now to be compassionate in the most difficult of circumstances. In the name of Lord Jesus, there is nothing which the power of His blood and the Holy Spirit cannot conquer.

Chapter Twenty-Three

I Learned The Importance Of Forgiveness

As the years passed, I learned more about the problems which family estrangement can cause. Understanding the underlying reasons for it helped me to heal the pain which followed. It can be defined as the loss of an existing relationship between family members, through physical and/or emotional distancing, often to the extent that, for a prolonged period, there is little or no subsequent communication between the individuals concerned. Violence might be involved, abuse, neglect or one or both parties' misbehaviour. I learned that the estrangement is mostly unwanted, like it was in the case of my parents, siblings and I.

I searched online for the meaning of 'estrange', and discovered that this is defined as 'no longer being on friendly terms with someone or part of a social group'. Just typing the next words, which add more to its meaning, fills me with sadness even now, as those I love suffered because of them, alienation, hostility, unfriendliness, bitterness, isolation, parting and division, I can relate them to my own life too, whilst to abandon, forsake, give up, quit and desert also brings back many unhappy memories. Across the years, witnessing aunts, uncles, cousins, nieces, nephews and siblings who refused to acknowledge or speak to other family members and us. The never to be forgotten slights made and received, tantrums and tears, often from when they were young. Some thirty or forty years later they could still talk about these events in great detail; the pain, disappointment and loss connected to them was clearly evident.

I didn't pay any attention, as a child, to the conversations I overheard on the doorstep, or when those who were technically estranged from us, felt brave enough to enter our cramped living room, before they poured out their loss and pain, always finishing the speech they made with a new possession or a special event they had attended. Instead I watched the impact this behaviour had on their relationships with others, friendships they made in the family, and at work. It was always someone else's fault which had to be talked about in a conversation with a third party, never a disagreement to be discussed or resolved with their own parents or the family members concerned. It was preferable to accuse the estranged person of madness, silliness, jealousy or negative behaviour.

Tiyanna and I often talked about the toxic experiences we had gone through in our lives, also the thoughts and behaviour which had caused them. The inability to forgive, pride, resentment, bitterness, jealousy, envy, gossip and the list continued.

What comes out of a person is what defiles them. For it is from within, out of a person's heart, that evil thoughts come. Sexual immorality; theft; murder; adultery; greed; malice; deceit; lewdness; envy; slander; arrogance, and folly. All these evils come from inside and defile a person.
Mark 7 : 20-23

I eventually realised that a generational curse had blighted my family, and I prayed with Tiyanna in Jesus' holy name for it to be broken.
"Do you think I came to bring peace on earth? No, I tell you, but division. From now on there will be five in one family divided against each other, three against two and two against three. They will be divided, father against son and son against father, mother against daughter and daughter against mother, mother-in-law against daughter-in-law and daughter-in-law against mother-in-law."
Luke 12:51-53

"Do not suppose that I have come to bring peace to the earth. I did not come to bring peace, but a sword. For I have come to turn a man against his father, a daughter against her mother, a

daughter-in-law against her mother-in-law. A man's enemies will be the members of his own household."
Matthew 10:34-36

I struggled at first in knowing whether to use estrangement or abandonment to accurately describe what had happened to us. The books and articles I read didn't differentiate between these two words, often using both of them interchangeably. However, being estranged could simply mean the relationship had dissolved or disintegrated. Each person had gone his or her own way without any animosity, hatefulness or playing emotional games. Communication and conversations had happened less as distance, time, work and family commitments took priority. Just as it had done in the case of my friends Candice, Brianna and I. How I wish it had been as simple as that in relation to my relatives, but emotional ties naturally run much deeper with family members.

On the other hand, I learned that abandonment can be distinguished by hurtful behaviour which might have originated in hateful comments, gossip, rebellion, being ignored or being excluded from events, both physically, and mentally. While the sole purpose of this behaviour, on the part of an adult son or daughter, was to be cruel, with the intention of making the abandoned family member or parent, the scapegoat. Ultimately banishing him, or her, the adult son or daughter usually held a core belief that the parent was guilty of a variety of shortcomings, and that any relationship between them would be harmful. Bitterness had set in, and the ensuing hatefulness eventually became impenetrable. Other family members and third parties fueled, encouraged or supported this behaviour which in turn encouraged the adult child to become more cruel, to cement this relationship. When its only strength was based on hate, bitterness, resentment and the inability to forgive the parent, the latter being considered mad, or quite simply jealous.

Anything positive in the adult child's life was rewritten as a negative. In the case of a black single mother educated in Britain, who had raised biracial children, it was easy for the latter to disassociate themselves from their African diaspora heritage, especially when they had European features. They could use the typical negative comments and attitudes attached to black females, despite the positive black role modelling of professional family members, and friends. Ultimately this wasn't any different to my second and third generation cousins, nieces and nephews who were again biracial, those no longer associating with their African diaspora family members.

Who wanted to be a darker skinned female? Where in society, social media, television, films or platforms had we been elevated, let alone treated equally or had someone fight for us? With my flat nose, thick lips, dark caramel skin and bald shining head, I didn't have a choice. I had to fight against the stigma created by my immediate family and friends, the supposition that I was useless, I wouldn't amount to much. I was sweaty, spotty and loud mouthed, whilst being physically abused, externally and internally. My mother and father slam dunked me, beating me hard with an electric cable, those solid, half-cooked dumplings flung at my face, along with boiling water, or whatever was at hand. My mother's twenty-eight stone body on my back whilst she trampled me. Yes, I was ugly, I fought at home and school. During my marriage, at work, and as I was being physically abused, I had to fight to beat cancer, the strokes I had, and being in constant pain much of the time. As a result, I didn't have any energy left to deal with my family's estrangement or abandonment. My life was already hard enough.

After a long time, I realised that there really wasn't any difference between the person I called the estranger, and the estrangee. These roles could fluctuate in the pain and loss suffered by both. In any relationship, the boundaries between the two were unclear. Sometimes the first person could be the estranger, and on a different day, the estrangee. We might feel that we had been abandoned despite being the one who had left. No matter how we described ourselves, we could still feel an emotional loss, and the impact of severing the relationship. However you look at it, family estrangement could be a hurtful process; it was intentional too. The abusive behaviour by the estrangee to the person who had been abandoned, was done with the sole aim of disrupting his or her mental health, and to inflict emotional abuse. It was sometimes as if I was walking on eggshells, not allowed to ask questions or give an opinion, even critique anything said or done, otherwise World War III began. You could tell this by the way the body language changed, he or she was watching the clock, huffing and puffing, with eyes rolling dramatically for effect. This became more pronounced when there was a large group of supporters present or in a public place. It was possible then for World War III to erupt.

Or it could be a case of silent treatment being given, not being acknowledged or receiving the benefit of good manners, despite the card or gift which had been sent. The other person had become incapable of responding appropriately. Again this was done with the sole purpose of inflicting emotional damage and psychological distress. False accusations were often made to belittle the other person, including me. Name calling took place; bullying, and gossiping about us. The adult child felt vindicated that the other was receiving his or her just desserts. It was payback time! They were now the King or Queen taking revenge, based on a falsehood of neglect and abuse; the wrongs which the other person had apparently inflicted on them in the past, all of which would now be shared with family and friends for their participation and enjoyment. They made sure that their children watched the performance, and were entertained by it. Although they were not asked to become involved, this humiliation was done publicly, privately or online, especially as a way of causing finger pointing and pain for the parent. Theft also played a part in this; sometimes it was money, property, pets, credit cards, or anything which the other person valued. It might have been done by means of forged signatures or tricking parents into signing an important document which was to their detriment, but for the benefit of the adult child, such as a will, deeds, loan agreement, power of attorney, intended to transfer assets or other property.

Embarrassing and difficult situations happened a lot, often by way of threats, intimidation, swearing, bullying, disclosing personal and private matters to a third party. There would be short and rude replies in any communication between the parties or the use of high pitched laughter, and scorn in public. A refusal to engage meaningfully by giving the impression to others that the conversation, and our presence, were untimely or unwanted. Then there was the deliberate damage to immediate family and property, threats being made to harm children or pets. Members of my family stole my cat while I was on holiday. When I reported the matter to the police, they told me that the issue wasn't about my pet being stolen, but more about effective communication!

The emotional blackmail which happened covered a wide area. This included withholding access to grandchildren, lack of emotional support when someone was ill, a lack of empathy or interest, wishing that the other person was dead. Threats were made to hit, smack, punch, pinch, bite, use physical restraint or other punishment, not forgetting the misuse of drugs, alcohol or forced sexual conduct. Looking back, it seems now as if almost nothing was off limits in the generational curse we suffered. *The Devil work ethic created division and dysfunctional cliques.* It all too often became impossible to ignore the carousel of bitterness and hatred which was going on around us. His part in the estrangement process was constant and relentless. He provided short term false foundations on which nothing good was going to be built. He also offered a choice of temptations, ranging from drugs and/or alcohol to numb the pain, money and temporary fame, or possessions which could also make us feel good at the outset.

It says in the bible that Jesus gives abundant life, and it can be easy to be nice to strangers, people we like, but showing kindness to those whom you dislike, cant stand or want out of your life is not so easy. We live in a world where right can easily be wrong so that wrong becomes right in our eyes. Thank you Jesus for removing the scales from mine. Hallelujah! Praise the Lord. *It is not for us to judge each other or condemn, but to forgive and we will also be forgiven.* When we blame someone, this means that we have judged them and will feel resentment towards them. This leads naturally to bitterness so that we will then dislike or hate the offender, creating rebellion, anger and revenge, or rejection if our anger is internalised, causing us not to feel good about ourselves, or be filled with self pity.

Forgive, and you will be forgiven. Luke 6:37

Chapter Twenty-Four

Healing The Past

When we blame someone, it is possible to escape from the pain by fantasising. This is usually followed by obsessive thoughts and confusion. On the other hand we may internalise how we feel. When this happens we can become anxious and afraid which can in turn lead to depression with feelings of emptiness, bewilderment, despair and hopelessness. This can cause obsessional behaviour which leads to a reliance on drugs, alcohol, the need to be accepted on social media and offline. People pleasing behaviour often follows this, entering into shallow relationships and opening the door to suicidal thoughts. Hopefully, not to the extent of committing suicide, but we may still wish to be gone if the pain is too great. People try in different ways to relieve the pain caused by not being able to forgive, but it is like putting your finger in a hose to stop the water from coming out. It is impossible to push water upstream, since it flows downwards. Ultimately the only way to resolve the problem is to return to where it started, cancel the blame, and forgive. The emotional pain and symptoms will then leave you.

In Colossians 3:13 the bible tells us to make allowances for each other's faults, and forgive anyone who offends us, as the Lord forgave us, we must forgive others.

For if you forgive other people when they sin against you, your heavenly Father will also forgive you. But if you do not forgive others their sins, your Father will not forgive your sins.
Matthew 6: 14-15

I found it easier later on to write down the names of those whom I had not forgiven deep within my heart; those whose words and behaviour had misjudged, snubbed, robbed, abandoned, rejected, offended, cheated, shamed or abused me, whether this was spiritually, physically, emotionally or sexually. Many people find it the hardest to forgive themselves, or even ask God for His forgiveness, so I asked the Holy Spirit to help me. I prayed and fasted for a closer relationship with the Lord, to pull down strong holds, greater faith, to be a true servant to those I meet – putting action behind my faith, doing, helping, supporting the vulnerable as I go along in life – giving back where ever I can.

As in Matthew 18:35, we need to forgive from the heart, to pray from our heart. The emotional pain we are feeling, and its symptoms, will then leave us.

My physical and mental health were severely affected by the shame and embarrassment I suffered after the estrangement of my family, pushing me eventually towards suicide. Cognitive behavioural therapy sessions with an oncology psychologist for two years, books, and online forums helped me enormously to survive and heal. Nevertheless, I still felt anguish and confusion because of what I believed I had done wrong. Re-evaluating my parenting skills as a single mother; begging for my child to live when I was seven and half months pregnant, while I lay in a hospital bed after being kicked by Adam, before leaving my marriage when that same daughter was only a few days old. Thinking that I should have stayed a little longer in that abusive relationship. Later studying full time and working to pay the mortgage whilst leaving my children in nursery and childcare every day, from early in the morning until seven at night. Not listening or giving them enough attention, and the holidays we had abroad always being too short.

I still don't have the answers to these questions, but I have learned that I must leave them behind. I can't change the past, only evaluate, and apologies for any mistakes I made. As I move forward, accepting the situation as it is, the majority of the pain I felt has gone, although I am still occasionally overwhelmed by it, and fall. I was able to heal only when I had accepted the past and learned to forgive, not only others, but myself too. Not everyone who is estranged can be a friend even if we share the same kinds of loss of family. It's best to look for solace in those places where we are most likely to find it instead of seeking it from people who can't give it to us.

I found it helpful to think about being creative, to find my own solution to healing. You might want to read books about recovery, and talk with others online about your suffering. Search for the most suitable forums, and groups. Choose one or create your own which is composed of people who have had similar experiences. Be cautious if you do this. Everyone has their own baggage in life, and people sometimes try to get their needs met by dumping this onto someone else; don't let them do it to you. This realisation led to me becoming aware of my own baggage, that it was safe to talk to some people but not others. Finally, I learned that we can't make someone else love, like or include us in their life, however much we might want them to do so.

I came to realise that the generational curse carried on because of children rewriting the past, without anything positive in it, such as the support, physical, emotional or financial help they had received from their parents, until they became adults and sometimes longer. Conveniently forgetting that their parents had sacrificed much of their own lives to raise them, and had often paid their school fees, The innumerable hours spent working to meet the mortgage on the property where they lived, holidays, driving lessons, and extra lessons to ensure they secured a place at university. Nothing like this, or anything else of a positive nature was acknowledged. Instead the 'curse' acted in such a way as to scapegoat, and banish those parents, using hurtful behaviour, along with a core belief that the parents were guilty of shortcomings, and any future contact with them would be detrimental to the adult children or their own offspring.

If the generational curse only affected one of the parents, then it seemed to be important to locate the absent one who had contributed the least towards the upbringing of his or her children, despite never attending a parents' evening at school, getting up during the night, or struggling to raise them. If there was also a step parent in place, again with his or her own children, this was even better. They would fit more easily into a new family unit. The partying which could be done, painting nails, grandchildren to fuss over, and sitting at the top table when there was a wedding. Not forgetting the endless outings they could join in, and award ceremonies or graduations to attend.

The battle lines were drawn for war! Even though there couldn't be any winners in the end, so far as the generational curse was concerned. I used to listen to and watch the prodigal children who had suffered because of this, pouring out their anger towards their parents and siblings. The comparisons and complaints soon turned to hatred, one upmanship and gloating about what they had or planned to do. Often spoken of scornfully, or in a mocking tone of voice if they were corrected or reminded of something positive in their past by the alienated parents. This was quickly followed by silence, shrugged shoulders, or nervous laughter, with a long drawn out example of something unrelated being given to replace it. If there hadn't been any physical abuse, they would include a detailed account of an emotional or other physical experience they had, adding this to any pleasant memories which might have been mentioned, captivating those who were present with their own story. The prodigal children had already chosen their parents' enemies, so that it was unlikely they would disagree with them, especially if the children had influence, success and money.

You have already seen the effects which the generational curse had on odd family members, but it became a whole new ball game within my marriage when I saw it being played out physically between my step-daughter and Adam, her father. I watched while estrangement destroyed their relationship, with innumerable allegations and Court litigation. This resulted in them not having any respect, loyalty or trust for one another.

However, I couldn't help but secretly wonder sometimes if I would one day become a fully estranged parent. It had happened to a few of my relatives, and I had also suffered a partial estrangement at their hands.

Why Can't You Be Like My White Parent?

Only a handful of words, but which had cut me like a knife when I was being compared to Adam, their father.

All biracial children, if they have European features, are considered to be the most beautiful. Biracial children who do not have European features walk a different road to their peers. Adam was my complete opposite; white privilege oozed from him as soon as he entered the room. He was incredibly wealthy. He had an excellent private education, drove a Bentley and smoked cigars. A businessman whose homes included a manor house in the country and a luxury three bedroom townhouse in central London, his cleaner, cook, gardener, chauffeur and accountant were all on speed dial. He had never caught a bus, train, or gone shopping in the supermarket. Nor had he changed a nappy as all of his children had nannies and went to boarding school. His financial status meant that he didn't have to run outside in the freezing cold to top up the gas or electric meter.

After our divorce, I watched my daughters leave in the back of the most expensive and up to date high performance cars. They absolutely loved it. The time they spent with their father was fun, fun and more fun. The Guardian ad litem, writing his report during our many contact disputes, said that we were poles apart: "The Father is laissez-faire whilst the mother is proactive, routine." I could see the sadness in the girls' faces when they came back to me. I was a single parent, and couldn't offer them the same lifestyle as he did. When I left Adam and we were still living at the hostel, the other women and I used to watch while the girls' expensive outfits were taken off on the drive, and replaced by the clothes they had worn when they had been collected. Two parents. Two different races. Two children.

Why can't you be like Dad?

It's so hard to deal with the personalities God gives our children whether saint or sinner. It is more than we can handle and I remained mystified where this came from, even astonished at some of the things they did and do.

I thank God for Jesus, His patience to deal with my melt down and the comments and behaviours of my children, but this IS parenting at its core. No booklet was given at birth, no guide, no instructions with these new born babies but God's Grace and Mercy to cope, guide and raise them. I can't offer a quick fix solution, write about the harsh words and actions – but I can tell you about prayer daily, trusting, believing that nothing is too hard for God, the eventual turn around, maturity, love and forgiveness. Each time the past is mentioned, I use it as an opportunity to praise the Lord on his input and moving forward, and the blessings he has provided for us as a family.

I have come now to accept this as another part of my healing process after the power of the generational curse went far beyond the pain I suffered because of chemotherapy, or inside my bones. This time it touched my soul. It was only through the entrenchment of sin, and the blood of Christ that I was able to forgive these thoughts, and get on with my life again. As always, the answer was to hold onto Jesus, and to not stop praying for the good outcome, which did eventually happen. My daughters were both at university and doing well by the time I started writing this book. The Devil and his generational curse no longer had any power over us. We are a loving family, happy to spend time together, with Mom-mi too ish!

Chapter Twenty-Five

Support From Friends

So much thought has gone into writing this book, and remembering the people who have come and gone from my life; how my relationships with others changed across the years, as I did too. The friends who were important to me, and two in particular who helped me get through some of the most challenging times. My thoughts drifted back to the restaurant where we used to meet, and I glanced around as I waited next to the reception desk to be seated at a table.

I was looking forward to lunch, but not the conversation I was about to have. The waiter smiled at me before I followed him to a table near the window. While he watched me squeeze into it, I smiled at him. He looked amazing, and my eyes didn't leave him until he had disappeared from sight. I settled myself in, expecting to have a long wait. Chandice and Brianna weren't the best at being punctual, but I was used to it. I could see most of the restaurant from where I was sitting so I had plenty to entertain me. The cooked meats, salad and French fries on the plates at the next table made my mouth water. The restaurant was buzzing beneath the bustle of lunchtime activity and the lingering aroma of good coffee. Rising and falling noise levels were interspersed with bursts of laughter. I could hear the orders being left at the bar in high and low pitched voices. Waiters skillfully navigated the crowded seating areas, as if gliding on ice.

Mine had asked me with mischievous eyes if I would like a glass of rose, and he soon appeared with it. I kissed my teeth softly at him before taking a long gulp of the wine, and he was gone. Other waiters scurried past my table, with an endless stream of customers, some of whom had paid the bill or were being seated, shaking coats and stamping their feet as if it had been raining in here. I glanced through the window at the people on the pavement outside. By the time I had almost finished my wine, I was starting to feel anxious.

The women I was waiting for had been my advisors, critique and prayer partners for a number of years, also good listeners to whatever I told them. Our friendship had been filled with honesty, humour and support. All of the embarrassing and serious situations I faced in my life, nothing had been off limits, whether it was children, family relationships, work, business deals or finances. They knew it all, but I had started to feel as if there was something wrong. We met only three or four times a year, and spoke to each other in the meantime as little or as often as we needed to. This meant that sometimes we didn't contact each other at all, we also had different friends. We didn't even know each other's siblings, family or work colleagues, mostly I guess because we lived a considerable distance from each other, so we were unlikely to meet, unless we had specifically arranged it.

Our friendship began thirty years earlier when all of us had careers in education. There had been a lot of changes across the years in the jobs we had, often with us becoming overqualified, and we experienced the black woman's person of colour challenges in these workplaces. We had collectively been demoted, promoted, overlooked or simply changed career paths. I had started to think that our main connection was through Christ; in prayer, and reading the bible but even that no longer seemed right. During our conversations, I sometimes felt that I had grown to value my faith more than they did, and meeting like this was too much of a habit, simply for us to bounce our lives off each other; not forgetting the sour experience we also shared of being the family scapegoat.

Chandice and Brianna were older than me. When we talked, they often began their sentences with: "Can't you see? I told you before to nip that in the bud. You are still putting up with that!" So I already had a good idea of what to expect from them that day in the restaurant. My stomach flipped, and I frowned in frustration. I didn't need this any more! I knew only too well what they would say to me while we ate, and drank wine. Even before we were well into the conversation, it wouldn't be difficult to tell from their facial expressions, and the rolling of eyes, what they were thinking of my latest escapades.

As they were still nowhere to be seen, my thoughts turned again to another interview I had years ago. One candidate stood out from the rest when I went into the interview room. I watched how she behaved towards the members of the panel who strode past us with a polite, "Good morning!" She was clearly on friendly terms with all of them. I sank further into my chair. Until that point I thought it was going to be a fair fight, but the longer I watched her I knew. My disappointment and exasperation must have been apparent; its voice was roaring inside of me amid the twitching and eye rolling of the other candidates who were also looking at her.

After a few minutes, I couldn't stand it any longer. I excused myself and walked into the toilet room which had four cubicles. It was cold and clean, a fresh smell of bleach and lemon disinfectant lingered in the air. The huge mirrors above the sparkling taps and small hand basins glistened, as the electric light caught them. I put my full weight on the basin, and stared into the mirror. What a waste of time this was. It had taken me an hour and a half to get to the interview, and it was perfectly clear now who would get the job. I could feel my heart sinking lower inside my chest. As I stared into the glass, one of the cubicle doors began to open, and the winning candidate left the end toilet with the lightest of steps; she was soon standing next to me.

Chandice Walker was stunningly beautiful. She had smooth, dark chocolate skin and large Egyptian eyes. At five feet in height, we were like little and large, staring at each other's reflection in the mirror. The tight cornrows in her hair were inside a neat bun, with a purple and blue strand running through it. She was thickly built, with broad shoulders. Her tightly fitting dark blue dress accentuated a high bottom and voluptuous curves. I came to the conclusion later that the main reason she didn't have any difficulty in attracting men was because she looked fabulous. I also remember admiring her patent shoes, as she sat opposite me in the waiting room with the other candidates. Even her feet were sleek and beautiful.

Chandice looked me straight in the eye through the mirror, and we both laughed; it felt so good at the time. The sound we made was loud, hard and wild. Hollywood stars would have paid a fortune for her brilliant white, perfect, teeth. Our friendship began that day, right there in the toilet. There was no need to say anything else, we had already bonded. I could tell that she understood this in the same way as I did. We agreed to meet at the end of the interview in a nearby MacDonald's cafe, and to wait for each other. True to her word, she did exactly that when she was told to go for lunch.

Chandice always seemed to try her best to make her relationships last, putting her heart and soul into them. She was highly motivated and organised, working sixty hours every week, she still spent a long time in the supermarket afterwards, buying only the best cuts of meat to cook for her men. She would clean their houses, redecorate them, pay their bills, give them hospitality, take them to shows and restaurants, while they cheated on her, and played around, living on marijuana and alcohol. We spent many nights looking for "his car" at two o'clock in the morning, parked outside the place where the woman lived whom he had met online for casual sex. All the tears, tantrums and game playing that went on back then. I didn't comment on any of it. I just listened. I was too afraid of saying the wrong thing, so giving her advice, for it to sink in took ages. Chandice treated her men very seriously.

Both of us had a sister who betrayed us with a husband or partner. Although in my case, I still wasn't sure if Adam had given in to the temptation, whilst Chandice had become extra careful who she introduced her partners to, if anyone at all. I felt ashamed to tell her the full adult version of what had happened to me. It wasn't long before our divorce, I had walked in on Elsey holding Laura on the stairs and playing with her, knowing full well that Juliet was upstairs trying to sleep with Adam. Something had made me turn the car around that night and drive home. I heard him say no to her while I stood in the hallway outside our bedroom door. I left the house shortly afterwards in a rage. I wasn't able to forgive either of them when it happened, and for a long time after our divorce.

The biggest flaw Chandice had was that she was a giving person, and those men certainly took from her, time and money. They inevitably left with another woman who did little or nothing for them. They nearly stole her mental health in the process, but she didn't create any barriers to protect herself or guide her heart. I could see all the signs of my past relationships in what was happening to her, so I kept quiet, just sat there looking glum.

Her endless stream of boyfriends caused enough drama in her life to rival a television soap opera. We lived in an intense world of driving around dark streets at night, stalking mistresses, wives she didn't know anything about at the start, and a multitude of other women. Chandice eventually got caught with the keys to an ex- partner's apartment in her pants. After he cheated on her, she decided to take revenge. She had stripped his flat of all its furniture, and on another occasion, left one partner in a parking space with a seasoned joint. I can't believe now that we did any of this. One night we even ended up following more than one of the men at two o'clock in the morning, just to see where they were going, and listening to their lies afterwards. Somehow she didn't learn from these experiences, and carried on picking the wrong ones.

Brianna Clarke was the other friend I was waiting to have lunch with. She and I had met while working at the same school a few years earlier. I was leaving just as she was walking into the staff room, intending to collect her mail from the teacher's cubicle. She had a quiet disposition with a soft African accent. She stood tall in a red dress and had shoulder-length braids with pink rouge on her cheeks. Her face was caramel in colour, round and warm, yet my overall impression that day was how unhappy she looked. She was the same height as me, pleasantly plump and groomed to perfection. I felt she was maternal from the first moment I saw her. As a lawyer's wife and mother of five children, all of whom were successful in their own right, Brianna could understand the fall out which had happened between my Mother and I. She was a similar age to Mom-mi, whilst her children and grandchildren were closer to mine.

My instincts pushed me forward, without any hesitation. "Are you okay?" I asked, and we were soon sitting next to each other in the tiny administration cupboard she called an office. She began sharing her black woman challenges, as Head of the Department. She told me she was a devout Roman Catholic, and the prayers we said together that day were heartbreaking. Someone else wanted her job and clearly felt she could do it better than Brianna. All the petty game playing which had taken place made me think that some adults could behave far worse than innocent children do. The situation didn't improve after she left the job, her successor was given additional support, whilst Brianna had been doing the same tasks single handedly for over ten years. My bond with her became very special to me. Every time we met she used to analyse the issues I faced, and give me a five minute call. Her advice would often be to pray for those who had hurt me, then leave them.

By the time we were due to meet in the restaurant that day, she had experienced her own cancer treatment journey. Her only praise for God was to make the occasional comment that He had brought her safely through it. My own illness happened a long time after hers, again with God also bringing me through it. He sent the unlikeliest support to help me which proved invaluable when I was trying to cope with what was happening, and helped me change a lot of things in my life while I was recovering. I realised afterwards in prayer and bible study, that God had always sent someone. The conversations I had with Brianna became focused on how God had helped both of us overcome our challenges. She always advised me to bless my enemies, and try to see things from their point of view.

She also repeated my Mother's comments about the generational curse on the girls in our family, many of whom were broken. They had never experienced a stable relationship, cuddled or hugged anyone else. Neither had they found true love, or had children. Despite being well educated and homeowners, they passed from one relationship and job to another, time after time, climbing higher and higher in their social status. They had spent their lives listening and watching others talk about God; how He had given them, including myself, the strength to succeed, showing us along the way that it wasn't always about money or what we owned, but our relationship with Him which mattered the most.

Brianna told me that people like this didn't have the maturity, experience or blessings which I did. They despised me, treated me harshly, and ignored me because of it. So much so that I had become the family scapegoat. She said that scapegoats were more often than not the givers in life; they really did give what they had, whether this was time;,money, or physically turning up to help without seeking any reward for it. Both of us agreed that this was the true meaning of being a Christian.

One of the most fascinating conversations we had was about how parts of my life were like *The Princess And The Pea* fairy tale by Hans Christian Andersen, in which a young woman's royal identity was established following a test of her physical sensitivity. Brianna started talking about it first, but Chandice and I soon joined in. It took us in a different direction. The Prince wanted to marry a Princess but was having difficulty finding one who would be a suitable wife. Something was wrong with every woman he met. He could not even be certain that they were real Princesses. One stormy night a young woman asked for shelter in the Prince's castle. She also claimed to be a Princess. The Prince's mother decided to give her a test by placing a pea in the bed she was offered for the night; it was covered by twenty mattresses. In the morning, the Princess said that she had suffered a sleepless night, she had been kept awake by something hard in the bed which she was certain had bruised her. The Prince was filled with joy. Only a real Princess would have had the sensitivity to feel a pea through such a large quantity of bedding. They got married and lived happily ever after.

In real life terms, we decided that the tiny pea represented me, as the scapegoat or black sheep of the family, fragile;,delicate, kind and considerate, I should have been happy, with not a care in the world. However, I had been covered by twenty mattresses. Each one was akin to an obstacle which had hurt me. I had been disappointed, became a party to unresolved conflict, felt cheated, betrayed, involved in toxic family issues, and I had lost my job. I also had financial worries and experienced a delay in reaching my goals. The list was endless, with all of this on top of me, that tiny pea, as I navigated my way through life.

It is only natural to experience a fight or flight response when we are exhausted. At the same time, we are supposed to be trying our best to get over the obstacles we face, and move on, looking for different people with whom we can share our lives, a new home, car, office or job, changing a partner or church, possibly not having any further contact with other people. That little pea has to carry a heavy weight, the entire world it is trying its best to navigate. After a single night's sleep, the Princess had the sensitivity to feel it, telling her hosts how uncomfortable it made her feel, and that it had bruised her.

We talked about this sensitivity, how it was my character being moulded and shaped through the weight of each mattress on top of me. I was fighting the obstacles without making any headway. Whilst this process was slowly changing me, my character and values, testing my beliefs and behaviour along the way, just the same as it had done during my depression. The Princess spoke about it when she said that she had experienced a sleepless night. As adults, we have become confused in so many ways. We may use only one part of our character and behaviour at Church, and another at work. Perhaps be unforgiving towards our family, or be respectful only to strangers, even possibly those of position and stature. Our heart, intentions and actions are confused. As the months and years pass by, what makes it even worse, is that the person concerned expects to live happily ever after without completely figuring out who he or she truly is. I was still carrying this sensitivity of character around with me, only for me to meet other people like Adam, who were also damaged and hoping to live happily ever after, whilst my friends had their own fairy tales to live.

Chandice and Brianna always listened to me and tried to reverse any awful situation I was in. They would ask me how I felt, before letting rip. After dissecting every microscopic detail of what had happened, they unpicked the nonsense I was going through, adding their own common sense with hugs, kind words, and advice to think about. It took me a long time to wean myself away from their support, but it couldn't carry on any longer. I needed to stand on my own two feet. I will always be grateful to them, and finally I just gave it up in prayer to the Lord Jesus Christ.

As black women, my two friends and I had a lot of similar experiences at work. When we used to meet, if any of us had an interview, it was very rare to see someone who was the same colour as us in senior management at the organisation we had applied to join. When I reached this level in my own career, I suddenly became "the black expert!" The person to go to for advice, ideas and suggestions when dealing with an employee who was the same colour as myself. From my point of view, I felt that this drew attention even more to the colour of my own skin, and didn't help me integrate. Diversity and inclusion training would have been a much better option for my employer to have pursued. It also soon became clear that I was going to have to prove myself for longer than my white colleagues and show that I was good at my job, before the more junior members of my team would accept me.

These are the same colleagues who would book an Asian or Caribbean night-out, love the music, food, clothes, identifying with "black culture", yet have no real interest in physically mixing with "black people" or want the nose shape, lip features or hair care. In fact, the unconscious bias was real. Yes, we are all biased, can jump to conclusions, think things that are not, but really 'learned attitudes, assumption, belief and stereotypes that exist in our subconscious and can involuntary affect the way we think and act.

The three of us suffered from a lot of microaggression at work which had made us feel uncomfortable, upset, or offended. However subtle or difficult it was to pin down exactly what was being done or said to cause this reaction. Nevertheless, this also meant that we were at times believed to be difficult to work with, overly assertive, even dramatic, or someone who quite simply didn't fit in. When I tried to respond in exactly the same way as my white peers had treated me, I was ignored. I could tell too that some of the junior staff were more comfortable being managed by a white manager.

My shiny bald head being a curiosity didn't help! I was continually asked about the wig, glue or hair I must have used now or in the past. I soon learned to keep my tone low, smile at work during adversity, and pull the person to one side later if this became necessary. I eventually came to the conclusion that all of it meant nothing. You could have the best policies and training for inclusion, equality and so on, but ultimately black and white people are like oil and water. I am who I am. I can't hide it, nor would I want to. You know the minute you see me, I am black, or if you hear my voice on the phone and then meet me in person to be told " I wasn't expecting a …….. Unfortunately, despite the passage of time, I believe there is still a disparity in the treatment received by those who are black; does equality exist?

It was interesting to read the independent review by Baroness McGregor-Smith in 2017, with a further review of the UK employers' performance in 2018, considering the problems affecting black and minority ethnic groups (BME) in the workplace. This report gave employers recommendations on how to improve diversity in their organisations. I sent copies of it to my former employers. I wrapped them in foil paper and underlined the inequalities which had been found in training staff, mentoring, recruitment and especially the summary of findings, looking at ways we could move forward. I received thanks for sending the review, and was encouraged to produce a questionnaire for BME staff. My intention was to help create the change which has been so desperately needed for many years; also to give a voice to the countless cleaners, cooks and low paid workers who may have been afraid of rocking the boat, especially since there was still not a large number of black faces in senior management back then who would have been able to support the change, and them.

Subsequently, the George Floyd incident and Black Lives Matter movement, together with the Covid 19 pandemic, have had a huge impact on companies and organisations attempting to be inclusive. This doesn't mean recruiting from one ethnic group and saying that's it or placing one black face in the background of an advertisement, but by doing a lot more, giving black people full access to all of the opportunities within their organisations, and allowing them to be fully integrated. I believe too that, if we are really committed to creating fair, diverse and inclusive workplaces, we need everyone to work towards actively and intentionally addressing the lack of representation of black leaders.

Chapter Twenty-Six

The Joy Of Sisterlocks

When I was a teenager my hair was given an American style called the Jerry Girl. This involved hours of going backwards and forwards to wash each section of it in the kitchen sink, straightening it then using hundreds of tiny hard rollers shaped like perforated rods. These had an end paper and gave the hair a curly effect. The problem was that Mom-mi did our hair in between clients so it took a long time. If the perming solution was left in my hair for too long it became straight and dry, making the curls break off.

The biggest disadvantage to having Jerry curls was that they had to be kept moist after a special gel had been used. This always felt heavy, and gloopy on my head. It dripped down my collar, face, neck and clothes, leaving a permanent shine on my face, and greasy patches on my pillows, despite my having to sleep in a shower cap to keep my hair moist. The only thing I really liked about having a Jerry Girl style was that my hair felt soft and manageable afterwards. The greasy solution Mom-mi used was partially responsible for the ice pick,and bridging scars I had. I was constantly picking my skin afterwards, causing these scars to form.

I also had a large black dent in my forehead, from the endless rocking I did to comfort myself before falling asleep. I acquired this habit shortly before I started secondary school. I felt traumatised because I couldn't go to the same school as my best friend, Angelica; she was everything I wasn't, beautiful, short, carefully made up, with the latest hairstyle and clothes. She used to let me touch her hair which was long and curly like Michael Jackson had his whilst I was covered in hair on my chest and chin hyperpigmentation. The other kids used to stare at my face, fascinated by it. I overheard them talking, giving others the eye.

The hair under my arms was thick, dense and visible through my blouse. I was so conscious of this that I would spend hours picking the scabs which had formed, usually after I had been excluded or left out of the group. After a while, the others made a type of dance out of me, mimicking how I shrugged my shoulders, picked the skin under my chin and exaggerated my all over itching.

I had every treatment possible across the years to try and get rid of the scars and my ingrown hair - Laser sessions, punch excision with sutures, dermabrasions, chemical peels, fardel, even micro needling. All of it was expensive, and none of it worked. Only the chemotherapy I had as part of my cancer journey was able to stop, and heal my years of acne scarring. I always wanted to be kissed passionately under my neck, instead of having to wear scarves, keep my face down in photographs, or not being in any at all. Even now I am still conscious of the marks this scarring has left.

When I was in a relationship, the subject was strictly a no-go area, so not discussed. I wouldn't let anyone else touch the scars. My daughters found it strange, using tweezers for hair removal. I would give them a target of thirty to forty hairs, and they used to focus on the ones which had been missed in waxing or threading. This started out as simple curiosity on their part, but they soon let me know how much they hated doing it, nipping me with the tweezers, pulling at my skin or focusing on the other things I needed doing. I didn't blame them when this happened.

However, everything changed again when I was undergoing chemotherapy and discovered Sisterlocks, a natural hair care system. I noticed a young woman who had them at my checkup with an oncologist in London. I asked her a lot of questions in rocket time; I was so excited that I made the mistake of trying to touch her hair. This was understandably met with a refusal and a request not to. I assumed that it would cost a lot of money, but I still wanted them. Low maintenance would mean spending less time on my hair, not having to use a wig or glue. I could also grow it longer and have a variety of styles.

There was definitely no going back once I discovered Sisterlocks that day, and found all the information I needed online on their website. I learned from the main website I would never again need to use oil on my hair, which would be fantastic. I looked at the photo gallery, the loctician, and consultants' list; I also read about Dr. JoAnne Cornwell, the founder of Sisterlocks. She recommended that I find a good loctician who had been properly trained, and knew how to use the specialist tool which could install just over four hundred locks. I would also receive a starter kit to register them.

As Sisterlocks were expensive, I was expecting to walk into an upmarket hairdressers in Chelsea, where a glass of prosecco would be on hand, quality magazines spread out across a low table, with lush towels, and shiny floors. The loctician I consulted would be highly professional, with his or her name on the prestigious list which I intended to scrutinise before booking a consultation. Nevertheless, things didn't work out quite like that. When I telephoned several salons, I was given a variety of prices, before I had even met the loctician and she had the opportunity of giving me an even higher one. I discovered afterwards that if I had been recommended by one of their friends, then the price would have been a lot more reasonable, whereas, for a complete stranger like me, they felt able to ask for a ridiculous amount of money; this worried me. Although the locticians on the website had undertaken the training course, their actual work wasn't rated so my experience could easily have been a hit, or miss.

Once I had my tester locks which measured one and a half inches, I felt as if I was at long last falling in love with my hair. I still can't believe that for many years of my life I literally had a bald head. Wherever I was posted in the army or lived in the United Kingdom, I used to walk into a barber's shop and ask for all of my hair to be shaved off. I didn't give it the opportunity to grow. Even during the twenty-one day gap between my chemotherapy sessions, I would still visit a barber to make sure the one millimeter of growth was removed. The decision to have

Sisterlocks happened during my oophorectomy, while I was recovering from a pulmonary embolism, and I just loved the thought of it. My children hadn't seen me with hair; the only hair they knew I had was when they were given my tweezers and asked to remove the rogue ones.

After I had the tester locks for a while, I was told to make another appointment for a full installation of Sisterlocks' hair. I was so excited when I was due to attend the salon again. I arrived with my magazines, headphones and a flask. I had been warned that it could take between ten to fifteen hours to install the parting. Sitting in a chair for this length of time wasn't going to be easy, but I believed that the results would be worth it. I was right. I felt amazing as soon as I had my Sisterlocks. They were a massive boost to my self confidence and gave me a more positive outlook on life.

I received lots of compliments, and it was generally a low maintenance style. However, the locks could unravel in the early stages, thin, or even break if left too long before my retightening appointment. Mostly though, I thought they were a life changing experience. They helped me to heal physically, also showed me how to embrace my heritage and discover the beauty of having natural hair instead of shaving my head and believing my hair was unmanageable.

I couldn't help thinking that I should have had them sooner, but my faith in God has taught me not to have regrets. Nevertheless, I was tired of searching for a hairdresser who could do my hair, usually in a cold back room, with her taking endless breaks to answer the telephone, feed the family, serve another customer, or even nip out to the shops. I tended to itch all over when I was in a crowded space, and with a hairdresser who knew I couldn't go anywhere else, once she had started the process. There were also inevitable appointment changes at the last minute, being expected to pay more if I dressed well, spoke nicely or had an expensive car. If the hairdresser's own hair looked nice, and I asked for the same style, I often left the salon with something completely different. I began to feel intimidated, as soon as I sat in the chair. Is it wise to criticise the hairdresser working on your hair? I didn't. Instead I listened to a lot of life stories and questions about whether I could help with this or that, while she tried hard to find out where I had been before she did my hair.

When I think back now to all the attention my Mom gave to those wigs, using her press and curl tongs, and a comb heated on the small campfire we had. The way she could flick the curls, or slowly straighten the hair. The smell of it from the dry heat smoke wafting through the house. The time and dedication she put into her craft, and the care she took of her tools, putting them away behind the Singer sewing machine, wrapped in newspaper and plastic bags piled high on top of each other. All this, before telling us that we could buy our chips. Changing my beliefs about my hair led me to think differently about who I had become, the woman I was; it was my way to be kind to others, so why not myself?

When I began to do this, I found it much easier to forgive those who had hurt me. It was a slow process, but God once again had shown me the path, this time through prayer, and taking better care of myself. I will always be thankful to Him.

Chapter Twenty-Seven

Jesus Will Always Be With Me

During one of our conversations, Brianna mentioned Tar Baby from the Brer Rabbit stories. Chandice and her understood the reference to it, but I didn't. I couldn't remember what had happened in the story, so I asked for the short version of it. Basically, Wily Fox played a trick on Brer Rabbit. He made a doll out of tar and left it on the side of the road. When Brer Rabbit saw the Tar Baby, he thought it was a person, and had a one sided conversation with it. The rabbit was concerned by the Tar Baby's silence. He hit the Tar Baby because of his frustration in not being able to communicate with it, and the tar stuck to him. He hit it again with his other hand and, as you might well imagine, this also became stuck.

"That's how we behave towards difficult relatives," Chandice explained. "We become stuck to someone with whom we can't communicate. We love them, but they can't see our perspective, nor can we see theirs. Rather than attempting to resolve the matter, we stop communicating as often as we used to. This eventually results in short examples of negativity. You probably have a Tar Baby in your life. Someone you can't talk to, but equally can't walk away from. A mother who whines, an uncle slurping his soup, or a sister flaunting her figure, maybe even a father who is still waiting for you to get a proper job, or a mother-in-law who wonders why her son or daughter married you."

These Tar Baby relationships mean that we are stuck together, but in reality falling apart. All of us are inherently flawed and broken; perfection is beyond us. The situation is similar to being crammed in an elevator with people thrust together by chance on a short journey, saying as little as possible. The only difference is we will eventually get off the elevator, and never see the others again. This isn't the case with a difficult relative. There will usually be family reunions which you will both attend, maybe at Christmas or Thanksgiving; also weddings, funerals and so on, with both of you holding your breath, wishing for it to be over.

I was fortunate to learn a lot about healing from the books I read. In 'Irregular People', Joyce Landorf talks about a woman in her thirties who discovered that she needed a mastectomy. Her mother and she didn't communicate well with each other, so the daughter was reluctant to talk about it. One day over lunch, she decided to tell her. "Mother, I have just found out that I am going to have a mastectomy."

The mother was silent at first, and the daughter asked her if she had heard. The mother nodded her head, then she calmly dismissed the subject with the comment that her other daughter had the best recipe for cow foot soup.

What can you do when those closest to you keep their distance? When you can get along with others, but your family and you can't? I could easily relate to the above example. No one in my family except for Mom-mi, and later Juliet, mentioned my cancer, asked me how I was, or sat with me at an appointment. If we met briefly, they would tell me how dark I had become, and how much weight I had put on, then list all of those who had died from cancer. As a grand finale, they would often say that they had put me on the prayer list at church. They didn't seem to realise how much this hurt me, at a time when I needed their love, understanding and support. Despite all of humanity's intelligence and knowledge of science, it seems to me now that we are still a very long way from being able to stamp out ignorance like this, and the pain it can cause to others. Later on, they would give me updates of some friend or colleague they were supporting, or remain top secret about their illness, whilst discussing mine.

I began to wonder if Jesus had anything to say about dealing with difficult relatives. Was there an example in the bible of him bringing peace to a family whose members were in pain? When I asked these questions, I realised that the answer was his own, quoting those who had criticised Jesus, Mark tells us in chapter

6 verse 3 that he was the son of a carpenter and Mary; also the brother of James, Joseph, Judas and Simon, his sisters were there too.

Jesus went to the synagogue where he was asked to speak. The people were proud that this young man from their town had done well, until they heard what he said. He referred to himself as the Messiah, the one who would fulfil prophecies. Their response was that he was Joseph's son. Wasn't He? Not a Messiah! He was just like them. Nowadays we might have talked about the plumber's son or daughter from down the street, or the accountant on the third floor. Maybe the builder who used to date your sister. One minute Jesus was a hero, and the next a heretic. Those same people forced Him to leave the town. They took him to the edge of the cliff on which the town was built, intending to throw him from it, before he walked away.

When Jesus was in trouble, his brothers weren't there. However, this wasn't always the case. There was a time when they spoke, and were seen with him in public, not because they were proud of him, but ashamed of him. *His family ... went to get him because they thought he was out of his mind. Mark 3:21.* Jesus' siblings actually thought their brother was a lunatic. They weren't proud of him, they were embarrassed. You can imagine the comments made at the time:

"He's off the deep end, Mom. You should hear what people are saying about him."

"People say he's loony!"

"Yeah, somebody asked me why we don't do something about him."

"It's a good thing Dad isn't around to see what Jesus is doing."

Hurtful words spoken by those closest to him, and there were more:

His brothers said to him, "You should leave here and go to Judea, so your followers there can see the miracles you do. Anyone who wants to be well known does not hide what he does. If you are doing these things, show yourself to the world."
John 7:3–5

We can see from this that even Jesus' brothers did not believe in him. Listen to the sarcasm in those words, they drip with ridicule. How does Jesus put up with them? How can you believe in yourself when those who know you the best clearly don't? How can you move forward when your family wants to pull you back? When both of you have different agendas? What do you do?

Jesus gives us some of the answers. Knowing that we are weak, insane or unsure should inspire compassion for ourselves. Also kindness in others, even small acts of kindness. Knowing how to reveal our vulnerability and brokenness is the bedrock of true friendship. Not things, people or places, the latest gadget, house, car or job; instead the time spent with people. The alternative to perfection isn't failure, but to make our peace with the idea that each one of us is good enough. Good enough parents, siblings, workers and human beings. Only the Lord can love you the way you are, with the capacity for complete love during our less impressive moments, and to bestow forgiveness on us for our natural weaknesses.

I learned from my Bible research that Jesus didn't try to control His family's behaviour. Nor did he let their behaviour control him. He didn't demand that they agree with him. He didn't sulk when they insulted him. He didn't make it his mission to try to please them. All of us want the perfect family and friends, having the expectation that our dearest friends will be like our next of kin. Jesus didn't have this; look at how he defined his family:

My true brother and sister and mother are those who do what God wants.
Mark 3:35.

When Jesus' brothers didn't share his convictions, he didn't try to force them to do so. He recognised that his spiritual family could provide what his physical family didn't. If Jesus himself couldn't force his family to share his convictions, what makes us think that we can do this? We can't control the way our family responds to us. When it comes to the behaviour of others towards us, our hands are tied. We have to move beyond the naive expectation that, if we behave in a good way towards others, people will treat us properly. They may, or they may not; we cannot control how people respond to us.

If you let God into your life, He will help you. I can't promise that your family will give you their blessing, but I know that God will. Let Him give you what your family doesn't. If your earthly father doesn't affirm you, then let your heavenly Father take his place. How do you do that? By emotionally accepting God as your father. It is one thing to accept him as your Lord, and another to recognise him as the Saviour. Also, another matter entirely, to accept him as your Father. To recognise God as your Lord is to acknowledge that He is sovereign and supreme in the universe. To accept him as a Saviour is to accept his gift of salvation offered on the cross. To regard him as a Father is to go one step further. Ideally, a father is the one person in your life who will provide for and protect you whilst that is exactly what God has done, and continues to do. He provides for our needs: Matthew 6:25–34. He has protected us from harm: Psalms 139:5. He has adopted us: Ephesians 1:5. He has given you His name: John 3:1.

God has shown himself to be a faithful Father. Now it falls to us to be trusting children. Let God give you what your family doesn't if this is what you are seeking. Let him fill the void others have left in your life. Rely upon Him for your affirmation, and encouragement. Look at Paul's words:
"You are God's child, and God will give you the blessing He promised, because you are his child."
Galations 4:7.

I have learned that it isn't necessary to have approval from others to be happy, it isn't always possible. Jesus didn't let the difficult dynamic in his family overshadow his calling from God. Our lives can have a happy ending.

It says in the bible that: *the disciples went back to Jerusalem from the Mount of Olives.... They all continued praying together with some of the women, including Mary the mother of Jesus, and Jesus' brothers. Acts 1:12, 14.*

Those who had previously mocked Him, now worshipped Him. The ones who pitied Him, now prayed for Him. What if Jesus had disowned them? Or worse still, suffocated his family in demanding that they change. He didn't do this, instead he gave them space, time and grace, so that they could change.

I learned from this not to lose heart, and that God works in a mysterious way. He is still changing families, just like mine so that a Tar Baby today may become our dearest friend tomorrow.

And Peter said to them, "Repent and be baptised every one of you in the name of Jesus Christ for the forgiveness of your sins, and you will receive the gift of the Holy Spirit."
Acts 2:38

Baptism also became an important part of my healing process. It was not until I received my golden ticket to holiness that the full burden of estrangement was finally lifted from my shoulders. Lord Jesus literally poured into me like a flood, filling me with His Holy Spirit, until every worry, sad thought, feeling of shame and guilt was gone.

I will never forget when a small piece of paper advertising a local Church was gently placed in my hand, and the person who did this smiled at me; a golden ticket inviting me to hear the word of the Lord. I pushed it into my bag where it stayed until another one was given to me, inviting me to the Church, and reminding me that God loved me. Sometimes when we are in pain, we will try anything to make ourselves feel better, so I went to Church for several weeks. It had a small congregation which was friendly, and focused on the Lord. I used to go for two hours every Wednesday, always arriving on time. I would be taken to the back of the Church by the Bishop, and the Evangelist, who spoke to me about God, encouraged and motivated me, even prayed for my children.

I felt intimidated at first in sharing my journey with the Bishop. Nevertheless, he was a patient and kind man. He encouraged me to be baptised in Jesus' name, but I still felt uncertain. Having already spent sixteen years believing in the Trinity, now there I was, being told to repent. I had to be baptised by this Church in the name of the Lord Jesus Christ, and speak in tongues if I was to heal. So, had my Trinity baptism been done incorrectly? The Bishop held my hand and spoke to me in a soft voice. He told me that God had been with me in my home, he had heard my prayers. The Evangelist also said that God knew my heart, whilst I still thought that my belief in the Trinity was the right one.

But the bible tells us how powerful prayer can be.

The effectual fervent prayer of a righteous man availeth much.
James 5 : 16

Later that day, I suddenly felt the urge to pray. It came as a gut wrenching feeling, and an overwhelming loss of self control. My stomach, body and mind seemed to be floating, whilst my tongue moved by itself. I felt the presence of the Lord as I walked around my house in tears, screaming and shouting, Hallelujah. I spoke in tongues, an unknown language. I cried, gut wrenching sobs, as I lay wailing on the floor. It seemed inexplicable at the time but every problem, worry or concern suddenly disappeared. The blanket of depression had completely gone and my anxiety shifted, so much so that for the first time I felt free.

I telephoned the Bishop as soon as I could, and asked to be baptised. Within three days, it was done in the name of Jesus Christ. I invited my friends, enemies and family to the baptism. I wrote letters apologising to everyone I could think of. My home was totally cleared, as if in preparation for a new beginning. I had finally let go of the bitterness I felt in being ignored and excluded by others. All the childish incidents and insults; I simply let go of them all.

Three hours of speaking in tongues felt like five minutes; also the regular fasting and prayers which came later. I believe that God does hear our prayers, and I know now that He truly loves me. When I look back at all He has brought me through, I know too that Jesus was with me during every single moment of it.

My trials have become my testimony.

Epilogue

Challenging Seasons was written with love, and the belief that prayer can change our lives. If we ask, the Holy Spirit will help us. I think of my life now as a work in progress. Old habits, and routines can change with us, whilst we are able to use God's armour in its entirety for our protection. Today, I believe that everything that happened to me, was ultimately an important part of my healing.

This book is based on the realisation that I would need to live through whatever God sent during my lifetime. He showed me that He loved me, and the right path I should follow. He also gave me two beautiful daughters whom I love and both have done extremely well, and astonish me. God taught me how to live a good and fulfilling life through the lessons I learned; also, the true meaning of my love for Him and others.

Not my will, but thine, be done are important words I do my best to bear in mind during prayer. Helping the poor, sick, needy, feeding the hungry is constant prayer for us all. Even though God can make everything good in our lives, this isn't about us. It is, and must always be, about Him. His will to be done in His way, following His divine purpose. We may have a long list of things we want or imagine we need, and which we ask God in our prayers to provide. This may be easier than simply trusting in the Lord, but shouldn't we believe instead that what He wants will transcend anything we can ask for? *Ephesians 3:20.* Although it may not always be easy to have such a strong faith, as Jesus discovered in the Garden at Gethsemane during his crucifixion:
There appeared an angel unto him from heaven, strengthening him. And being in agony he prayed more earnestly: and his sweat was as if it were great drops of blood falling down to the ground.
Luke 22:43-44

If we desire to be at the heart of God's will from where it all began in Genesis, with His creation of the world; the light, and us... Is there any other way to pray?

I will leave you now... with God's most precious gift of all:

And now abide faith, hope, love, these three: but the greatest of these is love.
I Corinthians 13: 13

Challenging Season series:

Forthcoming Books
-Get off the bitter bus.
-What you need to know
-Know who you are

Contacts & comments…..

Jane_p51@yahoo.com